C000112709

FOOD THAT GROWS

A Practical Guide To Healthy Living with Whole Food Recipes

Tanda Cook, ND, and Sarah Marshall, ND

DEDICATION

For Justin, Barry, and Sarah
Kathryn and Bob
Thank you!

FOOD THAT GROWS.

Copyright © 2011 by Tanda Cook and Sarah Marshall. All rights reserved. Printed in the United States of America. No part of this book may be used or reproduced in any manner whatsoever without written permission except in the case of brief quotations embodied in critical articles and reviews. For more information, visit www.foodthatgrows.com.

FIRST EDITION

ISBN: 978-0615537375

Cover and Interior Design by Ben Fjare
Photography by Justin Cook

Without limiting the rights under copyright reserved above, no part of this publicationmay be reproduced, stored in, or introduced into a retrieval system, or transmitted in any form or by any means (electronic, mechanical, photocopying, recording, or by any information storage and retrieval system now known or hereafter invented) without written permission from the publisher. The scanning, uploading, and distribution of this book via the Internet or by way of any other means without the permission of the publisher is illegal and punishable by law. Please purchase only authorized electronic editions and do not participate in or encourage electronic piracy of copyrightable materials. Your support of the authors' rights is appreciated.

CONTENTS

CONTENTS

FOREWORD

Although the clearest reason for eating is hunger, our relationship with food is generally complex. Many of us struggle with over- or under eating at different times in our lives, and many of us recognize that food fulfills not only a physical need but often an emotional one as well. In general, our culture does not tend to value healthy food choices as much as it does ease of preparation and low-cost food items. However, for both physical as well as mental health reasons, it is important to be aware of your unique relationship with food, including your values around eating. Through increasing your mindfulness and intuitive eating practices, you will find that your body craves healthy, whole foods and that your desire for processed, mass-produced foods may wane entirely. As you nourish your body with healthy foods and become more aware of where your food comes from, it immensely increases the awareness of your place in the ecosystem, both as a consumer and a powerful agent of change. As the mind and body are inextricably connected, so are the practices of consciously eating healthy foods and nourishing mind and spirit.

Mindful eating essentially includes bringing your full attention to the practice of eating, including inner cues of hunger and satiety, as well as the food itself. It is generally the opposite of how many of us eat, gulping down some food item while we drive or type on the computer. Mindfulness requires that you slow down. It requires that you take a moment to pull your attention inward and notice how your body feels. It allows you to appreciate the sight, texture, and taste of your food and to prepare your digestive system to receive the food. And, it is very difficult to do in our daily lives! I tell my clients that we call it "mindfulness practice" for a reason. It does require practice. As you pull your attention back time and again to your food and the process of eating, it may

become more apparent how often you may eat. If we mindlessly feed our bodies, it is virtually impossible to improve our relationship with food.

My nutritionist colleagues have taught me about the concept of intuitive eating. It is essentially the opposite of disordered eating and dieting, where rules dictate what we are allowed to eat and how often. It is eating from the body instead of the mind, allowing us to eat what our bodies crave as opposed to what our minds tell us we should and should not be eating. Intuitive eating allows us to eat when our bodies are hungry and stop when they are satiated. Many of my clients will tell me that they do not know whether they are hungry and they do not know how to eat until they are full. Years of eating by the rules, whether of their own creation or from a diet or food plan, have taught them to ignore their bodies. How many of us have said to ourselves, "But I can't be hungry already, I just ate an hour ago"? This type of questioning of our bodies' own wisdom robs us of having trust in ourselves and our ability to eat. Without rules, many of us believe that we will be out of control with food. However, the wonderful thing about intuitive eating is that the more it is practiced, the more our bodies and minds become balanced and crave healthy, nutritious food. Once you learn to trust your body, your relationship with food also tends to improve dramatically.

Remember, as with any relationship, you must attend to it in order to improve it. Imagine the freedom in eating well, feeling acceptance and love toward our bodies, and having a balanced relationship with food.

-Kim Lockwood, MA, EdS, LCPC
Bozeman, Montana
June, 2011

PREFACE

"Our food should be our medicine and our medicine should be our food." – Hippocrates

Two years ago, in Bozeman, Montana, we opened our naturopathic medical clinic, Clearwater Healthcare; and so began the greatest, most challenging, and most fun adventure of our lives. We quickly became aware that our greatest passion was in educating people about healthy living through good food and balanced nutrition. As a result, we knew it was time to create a book that broadened our reach beyond Montana to every table in every home.

In the spring of 2010, we got a booth at the local farmers' market in Bozeman, Montana. Originally we had thought we would do health exams or pH testing or take blood pressure, but then we thought there had to be a more exciting way to spend three hours a week.

What to do with a corner booth, exposure to thousands of people, and a Tuesday night mountain sunset? We thought food would be a great idea. Not only food, but cooking demonstrations, and not only cooking demos, but handing out samples and recipes for free. We would educate the public on local, seasonal cooking and how to eat whole foods. We loved the idea.

Now to pull it all off…

We invested in an elaborate camp kitchen to be set up on site, a throwback from Sarah's days as a river guide, and we enrolled the farmers to donate food to us so we were sure to support local, seasonal foods and farms. The drill: We would call the farmers on Saturday afternoon and ask what they were harvesting that week to bring to market. They would tell us. Then we would sit together on the porch, in our office, or around the table and make up recipes to complement what was coming out of the field or off the butcher block. We'll never forget the night we did grilled leg of lamb with the rosemary wine glaze. We had been given a whole, bone-in leg of lamb from Montana Highland Lamb and had grilled it to perfection. We carved it all,

right then and there at the farmers' market; the table was surrounded by wide-eyed spectators watching Tanda carve a seven-pound leg. And then all of the hands reaching out to taste the results. People were licking their fingers and in awe.

Every week was a different game. We would experiment with recipes, taste-test, use our friends as guinea pigs, and fall in love with the flavors that were pouring out of our kitchens.

Then we would go public.

Every Tuesday night, after the farmers' market, we would look at each other and giggle about what we had created, the lives that we touched, and the doors we blew open in people's worlds regarding how simple and delicious good food can be. As the season wound down, our regulars were requesting two things: a cookbook and cooking classes.

The cooking classes we wrapped up into a Dinner of the Month Club where people would come to Tanda's house and watch us cook while they munched on appetizers, sipped on some wine, and asked us questions regarding health, food, and cooking tips. We would design the menu according to what was in season, what the crowd wanted, and what sounded good. We watched as more recipes poured out of our kitchen. Then, in the spring of 2011, it became increasingly obvious that we had the serious makings of a great book.

For years we have been thinking that we were going to publish a book. We never dreamed it would be a cookbook. We never dreamed that over the past ten years we would fall in love with food, cooking, and growing food as much as we have. This book is a slice of our lives, who we have become, and how we live health everyday. It's our hope that this book becomes a resource from which you can learn how to think about food, how to play with food, and how to weave a little love and fun into the kitchen.

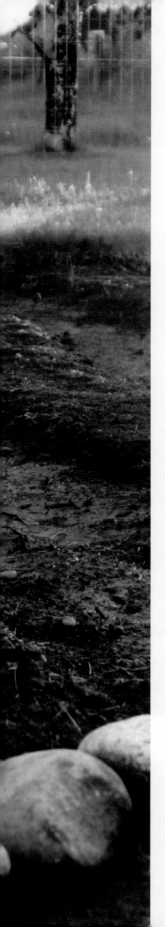

ACKNOWLEDGMENTS

We would like to thank, first and foremost, our incredible, supportive families. Without their foundations of love and inspiration to do great things, we would not be where we are today.

We would also like to thank Tanda's husband, Justin Cook, for his unwavering commitment to our success, donating time, photography, and patience. Thank you for enduring all the seven-day work weeks, evenings away from your wife while she was off at the market and the taking over of your house for dinner party after dinner party.

To the Barefoot Gourmet, whose culinary creativity has been the inspiration behind so many of these recipes. Thank you for feeding, and nourishing us with your and fearlessness to adventure with food. Your creations will forever be the ones by which we measure ours.

To Dickson Thom, ND, our greatest teacher, mentor, and physician, thank you for breaking the trail in practicing traditional naturopathic medicine, laying the foundation for this work. This book would not be possible without you.

Thank you, Kim Lockwood. Thank you for your mentorship, friendship, and professional support. Thank you, Kathryn Fiske, for your editorial skills, grammatical precision, and steadfast love and conviction in our success. Thank you, Robert Ruppenthal, for your relentless dedication to support our greatest impact on the planet, holding us accountable to our vision and mission.

And a few we have not met yet but would be remiss not to acknowledge their influence and inspiration:

To Jamie Oliver, for speaking out and inspiring Americans to revolutionize what and how we feed our kids. To Sally Fallon and her daring, cutting-edge book about politically incorrect nutrition and a return to a traditional way of eating that our souls recognize as food. To Michael Pollan, for his courage in boldly addressing the topic of where our food comes from and the interrelationship between food, agriculture, and culture. To the late Weston A. Price, for being the pioneer in the study of nutrition, how it affects our health, and the proper care and maintenance of the body through choosing whole, traditional foods that will prevent disease and ensure a healthy population for generations to come.

INTRODUCTION

"Give a man a fish; you have fed him for today. Teach a man to fish; and you have fed him for a lifetime. Unless he doesn't like sushi. Then you have to teach him how to cook."—Auren Hoffman, Herald Philosopher

This book was inspired by the food that is in it.
When you hear the words health and food used together what do you think? Strange, bland, flavorless, cardboard-like food that will leave you unsatisfied and hungry? Well, if you take the challenge and use this book not simply as a cookbook but as a guide to live health, you will discover food that adds health to your life can be juicy burgers, bacon and eggs, butter and thick gravy over roasted chicken, skin and all. In short this is a book full of recipes and ideas how to eat meat and veggies three meals a day, seven days a week, all the while adding health to your life.

It is our mission to change the way we eat in America: to bring us back to the basics, knowing where our food comes from and how to eat sustainably for the health of our bodies and our environment. It is our desire that you use this book not just as a great set of recipes, but as a toolbox to learn how to live healthfully, every day, through what you put in your mouth. This book is not just about what to eat, but about how to live, eating fresh, whole, made-by-nature foods that not only cure and prevent disease, but also nourish body, mind, and soul.

Our passion is to bring people into a new way of being with food. This book is not about a "diet." This book is the how-to manual to eat whole food, real food, that creates and sustains true health. You can read this like a cookbook and follow every recipe to the letter, but our intention is to inspire a new way of thinking about food, cooking, eating, and how to share food around a table with people that you love. This book will bring consciousness to your grocery lists, your refrigerator, your health, and your life.

Food That Grows bridges the gap from the farm to your table with simple, easy recipes to add health to your family and your life. It is the culmination of sixteen years of study, sixty-two years of collective experience, and a million years of evolution all combining together as your personal guide to health and healing. At the most basic, molecular level, we are literally what we eat. We cannot be any other. And so we invite you to embark on a great journey of exploration of what is in your refrigerator, on your plate, and thus in your body. You will discover that this story is about so much more than simply food—it is about being nourished from the inside out to become exactly who you have always dreamed of being.

In Part I you will learn the "who". You will learn about us, Dr. Tanda Cook and Dr. Sarah Marshall, and how two naturopathic physicians came to write a book about food, nutrition, and nourishing your body with whole foods.

In Part II we describe the "why". Here we dive into what health actually is and how to best support creating health every day with your lifestyle. Although this is a book about food, we would be remiss not to include more information about how to support all aspects of your health through daily choices we make about exercise, breathing, sleeping, physical and emotional detoxification, and, our favorite part, play and the importance of enjoying yourself, not just for your quality of life, but especially for your health. In this section we also give some background on what whole foods are, and why a diet based on them is essential to maintain and restore health. We will describe the basics of food allergies and how they differ from intolerances, and why one would consider living a gluten-free, dairy-free lifestyle. The world of food allergies and intolerances is a huge and growing subject, and whole books could be and have been written on the intricacies of the molecular science of food, the immunological issues with food, and the pathological consequences of eating food that does not agree with your body. This is beyond the scope of this book, as it was our intention to focus on the practical aspects of how to "live health." We have included a resource section at the close of the book for you to further explore these subjects with some of our more influential and favorite resources on the subjects of food, cooking, nutrition, and health.

In Part III we include our recipes for success. This is the most significant "how to" section of the book in terms of thinking about food, eating, and organizing your life to be the most successful at eating whole foods. In this section you will find out how to stock a gluten-free pantry, seasonal grocery lists, tips on how to eat more vegetables, feeding kids whole foods, and whole food snacks. Our goal is to take the concept of adding health with food out of the theoretical and move it into the practical.

One of the most common responses we hear from our patients regarding shifting their diet to eating whole foods is "time". They say they don't have time to cook, prepare, and plan the way they perceive it is necessary to do so. First of all, if you declare eating whole foods will be hard and time consuming, then likely it will be. If instead, as we have done, you declare eating this way is easy, fun, and a great adventure into new territory, then it will be. That being said, we also challenge you to really think about how long it takes to make many typical processed foods – macaroni and cheese can be at least 20 minutes start to finish and most frozen pizzas are 20 or more minutes plus time to preheat the oven. Many of the recipes in this book can be made in twenty minutes or less of prep time. Yes, eating this way may take some adjustment in your thinking, and we've included every time-saving, make-your-life-easy tip we could possibly think of to make it as easy as possible. We changed our way of eating from processed to whole foods in medical school with an eighty-hour-a-week schedule. Trust us, it can be done, and this book will give you every tool you need to do so.

Part IV is where it all comes together: the recipes. We mostly organized them into courses: main dishes, vegetable sides, gluten-free grains, sauces, soups, salads, appetizers and snacks. We also included a specific section of breakfast recipes. When we recommend our patients remove gluten and dairy from their diets, their most frequently asked question is, "But what do I eat for breakfast?" A gluten-free, dairy-free breakfast strays far from the all-American staples of cereal and milk, bagels and cream cheese, and pancakes. We chose to raise breakfast to its rightful place at the table of gastronomy: first and foremost, right in front, as the most important meal of the day. It is deserving of its own section full of healthy protein, fats, and complex carbohydrates.

Every recipe is introduced with a story of its inspiration or lasting impression on our friends, family, and clients. We also include tips on how to combine it with other recipes for fabulous meals or how to make the recipe with leftovers from another recipe, speeding up cooking time. We make recommendations for other variations of flavors or ingredients, turning each recipe into many new options to try and experiment with. We also include health information with every recipe, describing the health benefits of a main ingredient, the merits of purchasing choices, and tips on how to eat and enjoy food in ways that maximize its nutrient value.

We encourage you to get creative and play around with combinations, flavors, textures, and colors. What's the worst that can happen? When we have encountered an unfamiliar spice, herb, or vegetable, we play with it, putting it on and in everything until we figure it out. We encourage you to do the same. Get brave. Get creative. Get simple. Get involved. And most importantly, have fun.

It is our hope that this book becomes a tool through which people learn how to think about food, how to play with food, and how to be creative and weave a little love and fun into the kitchen. Our wish is that this book lives on your counter, becomes your food bible, and inspires those who sit at your table.

Have a blast with it and enjoy every bite.

PART I

"We are indeed much more than what we eat,
but what we eat can nevertheless help us to be
much more than what we are." - Adelle Davis

WHAT IS A NATUROPATHIC DOCTOR?

As naturopathic doctors, we have been extensively trained in both modern science and ancient healing traditions. We attended a four-year, graduate-level naturopathic medical school and were educated in the same basic sciences as a doctor of medicine (M.D.), but also studied holistic and nontoxic approaches to care. We provide comprehensive care not only for the treatment of disease but also for its prevention. By using protocols that minimize the risk of harm, naturopathic physicians help facilitate the body's inherent ability to restore and maintain optimal health. It is the naturopathic physician's role to identify and remove barriers to good health by helping to create a healing internal and external environment.

Naturopaths are trained as experts in alternative therapies while leaning pharmacology and minor surgery as well. Along with a standard medical curriculum, we complete four years in clinical nutrition, homeopathic medicine, herbal medicine, psychology, and counseling (to be skilled in assisting patients to make comprehensive lifestyle changes in support of their personal health).

Our naturopathic training is based on six tenants:

- Utilize the healing power of nature
- Treat the whole person
- First do no harm
- Identify and treat the cause
- Prevention is the best cure
- Doctor as teacher

In our practices we specialize in the treatment of food intolerances, allergies, gastrointestinal disease, eating disorders, weight loss, mood disorders and infertility. It is our passion to assist our patients in making choices every day that result in health and not disease. We understand that it is one thing to be told what to do, and entirely another to learn how to do it. That is why our approach to health care includes extensive education in health, hands-on experiential learning opportunities, and an abundance of tools to support health and healing, including this cookbook.

TANDA'S STORY

I grew up in an old farmhouse in the middle of rural Vermont on four acres with gardens and streams, chickens, dogs, horses, rabbits, forts, and a limitless imagination that took my three siblings and me on wild childhood adventures.

And my parents? Hmm, the best way to describe them is…magic.

Mom is the voice of reason. She has never forgotten what it was like to be a kid, and has made all life's challenges something to work through, live through, and grow from, with grace and gratitude. She gave all four of us permission to be and do whatever it was we wanted. She filled our life with magic. We all still believe in Santa Claus, and Christmas morning still feels like it did when I was six. She encouraged imagination, play, and communication. She gave us permission with boundaries, and love without conditions.

And when it comes to food, we all joke that she can burn water, and although that may be true, watching her set the tables for the dinners that my Dad cooked was a work of art. She would create centerpieces and place settings that would give the whole table a sense of life and personality. They would always match perfectly with the meal and give the food a place to come alive.

My Dad, born in Tanzania and raised in South Africa, is the artist and the chef. He learned to cook from both his parents and the people who worked in their home while growing up in Kloof, just outside the city of Durban. And then—while a high school exchange student—he learned from his host family in California, whose Swiss-Italian roots exposed him to a whole new style and range of cuisine.

Growing up, Dad always had a garden that he would tend to, talk to every morning, and pay us to weed. It would explode in the summertime with reds and greens and oranges. Dad would fill baskets with tomatoes, beans, fresh herbs, peppers, asparagus, and rhubarb. Piles of veggies would be stacked in the kitchen and I could watch his wheels turning as to what to combine and create for our next meal.

When we sat down to dinner he would point out everything on the plate that came from the jungle of green out back. Freshly chopped herbs on the barbecued chicken, thick slices of heirloom tomatoes with huge leaves of basil draped across them and covered in coarse sea salt and cracked peppercorns, the pile of mesclun garnished with orange and yellow nasturtiums, all configured perfectly, colors and textures making our mouths water and our fingers dance around the fork with delight. The plate was his canvas and the garden was his palette from which he would paint. The four of us watched with enchantment as he would take the first bite, clasp his hands together as if in prayer, and simply smile.

As we got older, our house became known for food. Huge dinners were put on for our birthdays, soccer teams, Fourth of July, and then the "just because" dinner parties with the silver, china, and crystal. My friends would beg to come over on Sunday mornings for Dad's waffles with the bacon surprise in the middle, topped with his home-cooked maple syrup from the maple trees on our property. It became such a treat for me to sit on the counter, watching him chop and peel and stir. He cooks with such love, passion, and intuition. He cooks like an artist. He cooks to nourish not only his family and his friends, but his soul. It's fun to watch. The stories of my father's food are woven throughout this book; he is my inspiration and my mentor. My best food memories lie in the thousands of meals my Dad has served on the plates of the tables that my mom set.

It was then in late high school, in 1997, that I developed an eating disorder. I watched as my relationship to food changed, and it would be changed forever, albeit in one form or another. I became a vegetarian, much to my father's dismay. Cutting out an entire food category felt so good, something more I could control, and "being a vegetarian" was an identity that I loved. I could use all of the vegetarian-approved foods to feed my addiction to the chemical high of eating, like candy, soda, breads, pastas, and baked goods. I would wake up thinking of food, how

I felt in my body, and what I could and could not eat that day. I lived on candy and Diet Coke. My list of "safe" foods to eat grew shorter by the day. I struggled through college, hid my disorder from friends and family, and swore every day that today was the last day I would binge and purge. But the next day would come and I would do it all again. I had no balance. I didn't know what was hungry and what was full. I didn't know what a portion was. I couldn't eat without an exit strategy. It was all or nothing. My social life was affected; my relationships were compromised as well as my grades. I was slipping into a way of being that was so far removed from who I was that I would look in the mirror and hardly recognize myself.

Then, a best friend, and roommate took me by the hand one day and said if I didn't do something about this, then she would. She was the first person who had taken a stand for me that I heard. The very next day I called a nutritionist and my recovery began.

It was my journey through an eating disorder that led me into my search for bigger answers that the conventional medical world was not providing. Antidepressants and anti-anxiety meds were all they were talking about. Neither was an ethical option for me. I watched friends around me suffer from similar disorders and become numbed by drugs, and boxes of pills lived under their beds. And then what? After all the medications and seeing minimal results? There had to be a different way of working through this. What I didn't see happening but craved was someone asking the deeper question: why. Why had I turned to food for control? Why do some people develop an eating disorder while others choose cigarettes or get chronic migraines? Why bulimia and not anorexia or overeating? Could I ever totally recover? According to conventional medicine, the odds were slim to none. I was hungry for answers and I was hungry for knowledge about food, how it works in our body, what the best choices were, and how our relationship to food can add health to our bodies and lives…or take it away.

It was naturopathic medicine and the people I met through school, in 2005, that fed my love for nutrition and healing the body, and taught me how to fall in love with food again. I just hadn't discovered it all just yet.

In the fall of 2003 I spent three months traveling around South Africa to learn and visit my roots, and to meet family for the first time, family that in my past had only existed in photos and stories from my Dad. I now had family that I could hug and kiss and experience. While living in Cape Town with one of my father's best friends, I had the privilege to do a variety of volunteer work. I worked with a veterinarian in the impoverished town of Kialisha, where I connected with a boy, maybe seven years old, whose dog was sick, and he had brought her to the clinic. He and I spent hours together, and even with the language barrier we ended up drawing pictures in the dirt with a stick. We drew the United States, pictures of our families, our animals, and our friends. We smiled, laughed, and even cried together. I went back to the house I was staying in that night with a newfound clarity…I knew I had to work with people and that adding health and love needed to be a part of it. So I came back to the States and worked with an orthopedic surgeon in upstate New York, as I thought being a physician's assistant was my answer. Turns out it wasn't. But so many things about being in New York were. I had been working for a month or so when I ran into Justin Cook, a handsome and quiet guy, at the local gym. We had met years before through mutual friends, and here our paths were crossing again. He asked me if I wanted to go out that night with he and his friends. I politely declined and said maybe another time. The next day he called me after work and asked again. I agreed, and we have been inseparable ever since. We had only been together a week or so when I told him about my struggles with food. Without a hint of hesitation, he smiled, and in the most compassionate way, he simply said, "OK." I was shocked. He didn't run? He didn't make an excuse to get out? He simply said OK…and my body relaxed. My mind rested. And our journey together began. We started talking about marriage after three weeks. I was buying wedding magazines; my mother was giving him the family diamonds. We were engaged after only a few months, and every day of being with him is a true gift. He is my rock, my grounding cord, and my best friend. My life is enriched every day because he's in it.

We then spent nine months together, in New York, where I watched people come in and out of the orthopedic clinic with laundry lists of medications and chronic health issues, but few answers. I said to one of the physician's assistants that I loved people, I loved medicine, but I didn't like

4

hospitals, so where does that put me? "Have you heard of naturopathic medicine?" He asked. I shook my head. He put his hand on my shoulder and said, "Go Google it." I did, right then and there. I crept into one of the doctors' offices, and the first site that came up was the National College of Natural Medicine. I read the philosophy, saw that they had four years of nutrition classes, and I was hooked. I printed the application and filled it out that night. I was going to naturopathic medical school.

Justin and I were married the summer of 2005. A week after the wedding, we packed a U-Haul and were off to Portland, Oregon, to start our journey at medical school. It was the first day of orientation; I wore a baseball hat and sweats and sat in the back of the room, where I picked Sarah and two of our other soon-to-become best friends out of the crowd. Justin had come with me that day for moral support. I nudged his elbow and said, "See her?" He nodded. "I'm gonna be friends with her."

Sarah and I met later that day; we hit it off immediately, sharing similar passions about the outdoors and health. We became study partners, best of friends, and eventually business partners.

I was two weeks into medical school and a now very dear friend of mine took one look at me, seeing my acne and my weight, and said, "Tanda, you have to eat meat." It was as though I had been punched in the gut. "No!" I thought. "No way." I was a vegetarian; I could never let go of that. It's who I was.

I gathered myself, looked him in the eye, and I asked, "Well…why?" He then proceeded to tell me a story of a girl that was a vegetarian who had struggled with acne, as I did, and when she started introducing meat into her diet, her skin cleared. My acne had been a struggle for many years, and if I thought eating a steak would help it, then I'd consider giving it a shot. For my skin, I would do most anything…even eat meat. So on the way home from a barbeque one night, I said to Justin, "Babe? I think I want to start eating meat." I couldn't believe those words fell out of my mouth.

I was terrified that he would react in a way that would shut the idea down. I sat there, staring straight ahead, anticipating his reply. Without skipping a beat, or even turning his head, he said, "OK."

The next day I ate a chicken breast and stir-fried veggies.

Since then I have been eating free-range organic meat three meals a day. My acne is gone. And my health and my life are back.

So to survive the years of medical school, Justin and I started hosting weekly dinners. Any form of gathering was OK with me. Barbeques, Halloween parties, Easter dinners, birthdays, or just a Sunday night get-together with a big roast-of-something. It made my heart sing to cook for a group, drink a glass of wine, sit around a table, and listen to the noises of enjoyment and connection. I looked forward to them every week. I would scribble menu ideas on scrap paper, Google recipes, make grocery lists in the margins of my cookbooks.

It became so clear to me that I had become my father.

I saw that food was community; food was communication; food was celebration; food was art; and food was creativity. Food was life.

So after graduation we brought food to Bozeman, Montana, where Sarah and I founded Clearwater Healthcare. We see patients young and old. We coach people into health through food and lifestyle. Our focus is utilizing all of the senses. We have people touch, feel, smell, and taste health. It becomes an experience that they can take home and use over and over.

We host monthly dinners, and we have a booth at the local farmers' market dedicated to educating about whole foods, seasonal eating, and that food should taste good and it doesn't have to take all day. I often tell people that the fresher the food, the less you have to do to it. Cooking should be fun and, as my father would say, "Mmm, I love food, I could live on it."

All of this was created because of our love for people, food, and the art of bringing them together.

It starts with your grocery cart. Enjoy these recipes and cook on!

Dr. Tanda Cook, ND

Bozeman, Montana
July 2011

SARAH'S STORY

Born and raised in beautiful upstate New York, I learned the art of living close to nature, and thus close to health, from my incredible, inspiring, and very wise parents. My older sister and I were raised as barefoot, corduroy-wearing, vegetarian, Buddhist, hippy kids. For the first five years of my life, every vegetable I ate came out of our backyard. We played in creeks and waterfalls all summer, taking frequent family camping trips throughout the East. In the winter I was outside in the deepest snow I could find, preferably skiing on what I thought at the time to be huge mountains. I went to a magical school without walls, a Rudolph Steiner-type elementary school where I fell in love with learning. It was there I discovered my life's quest to understand deeper and deeper layers of how this mystical world we live in works and thus, where my journey to become a naturopathic doctor began.

My whole life I have found my greatest pleasure spending time outdoors in nature. I feel the most "me" in the natural world and find I am recharged, renewed, and revitalized there. For a long time it was all things mountainous. Then I explored big Western rivers churning in white water, and now I am exploring the coasts of the ocean.

As a young adult I was pretty much obsessed with downhill skiing, and it was this passion that propelled me West. At nineteen years old, two days after my last final of my sophomore year at the University of New Hampshire, I packed my life into "The Rooster" (a 1993 red Mazda 626), and my sister and I drove across the country to Moab, Utah, where I was going to begin my summer career as a whitewater rafting guide. I didn't, in fact, guide at all that summer. But what I did do was meet the friends who would eventually lead me to two of my dream jobs: as a downhill ski racing coach and a multi-day whitewater rafting guide.

That fall I headed north to Salt Lake City to continue my studies in chemistry at the University of Utah. Chemistry, for me, was the ultimate way to investigate how the heck this thing called life worked. To get down to the very core of it all and see how it comes together. To go from whole bodies to organs to cells to molecules to atoms, right down to wave particle probabilities of an electron orbital. It was so incredibly fascinating. It was my foundation in chemistry that has continued to supply me with my greatest understanding of how best to heal the human body—and what life is really all about. That being said, I was still a typical college kid, ultimately more interested in adventure, fun, and boys. As the temperatures dropped and the snow began to fly, I found myself with a full-time job teaching skiing at Snowbird Ski Resort instead of in class. I quickly figured out the ski-bum school schedule, taking winters off and going to school in the summer, leaving me free to ski one-hundred-plus days a year in the greatest snow on Earth. It was that first job in Salt Lake, teaching skiing, of all things, that brought me to the realization that, next to my understanding the mysteries of the universe, my greatest passion was teaching. A few years later as a river guide, this realization deepened as I discovered that what I loved most about the job was the quiet stretches of –flat-water between rapids when I could talk with my guests about natural history, geology, Native American mythology, and health.

It was there, sitting on the back of a sixteen-foot Avon Pro raft, that I found myself constantly coming back to the subjects of nutrition, homeopathy, energy medicine, the mysteries of the human body, and how our modern lives have become out of alignment with living in nature, our health, and ourselves. It was while floating down hundreds of miles of river corridors in Utah, Colorado, Idaho, and Montana that I inadvertently uncovered my truth: that I was a naturopathic doctor, even though at the time I had no idea that naturopaths even existed.

That discovery came intertwined with the discovery of my passion for cooking. The summer before my last year in college, a friend had invited me to join him to travel in Coast Rica for two months, which, being the adventurist I am, I gladly accepted. As the trip approached, he backed out and I found myself traveling alone, without knowing a single word of Spanish, in a foreign country for the first time. I spent my first month getting a handle on the language, living with a local family, and studying every day. While this was a rich cultural experience, it was, well, hard, and not nearly as much fun as I hoped. So I jumped ship and went to volunteer at a small, American-run ecology center in the mountainous jungle.

As a volunteer I had my choice of sustainable building projects, planting and weeding in their tropical vegetable garden, or helping out with the daily chores of supporting the other volunteers, namely, feeding them. Somewhat by default, not being attracted to any other opportunity for work, I began helping to make the daily bread, as I had never made bread from scratch before. Next thing I knew I had a twelve-hour-a-day job preparing the meals for somewhere between ten and thirty-five people. That feat alone would have been challenging enough, but living in the jungle added another layer of complexity. The true test was making everything from scratch, as we were more than three hours from the closest grocery store, and being sure we ate the food before the bugs and mold could.

I settled into a delicious, rhythmic routine. I'd wake at 6 a.m. and mix and knead bread dough for its first rise. Then two young, tan Costa Rican boys, riding bareback on horses, would hand deliver our fresh, raw milk daily, still warm from the cow. From this we made yogurt and farm cheese, saving a little for morning coffee. By that time I would have punched down the bread dough, kneaded it again, and put it back in the morning sun for its second rise.

Next, with a steaming cup of Costa Rican coffee, I would pen notes for the day's meals, taking my inspiration from one of several of the great cookbooks the center had on hand. The Moosewood Cookbook, Laurel's Kitchen, and the Complete Vegetarian Times were my staples. I also played around with and learned a great deal from an Indian cookbook, a Thai cookbook, and the cookbook of some vegetarian restaurant in

Seattle whose name has evaporated from my memory. Then the cooking would begin for lunch, the bread would be baked, the yogurt cultured, and two hours later our first meal would be served. Lunch dishes would be cleaned as preparations for dinner were already under way: sorting beans, cleaning veggies, and making stock, dressings, and sauces. Dinner would be served at 7 and dishes completed by candlelight at 9. Exhausted, I would fall into bed and wake to do it all again the next day.

I graduated from college that May with my degree in chemistry. Three years later than expected, I finally got a job as a river guide floating the Green and Yampa Rivers in Colorado and Utah. I was asked to return to the ecology center in Costa Rica as the manager for three months while the owners made a long-overdue trip back home to the States. I joyfully and gratefully agreed and fell right back into my cooking routine. This was the time I really developed my inner chef.

My mom swears I couldn't cook to save my life until I came home from Costa Rica. I don't know that I was that bad before, but there is nothing like doing something twelve hours a day for three months straight to anchor it into your bones. Although I have long since left my vegetarian upbringing, many recipes in this book have their roots in what I learned in my time cooking vegetarian food in the tropics. I believe all cooks find their way into a specialty. For Tanda, it is an incredible skill at grilling, roasting, and toasting just about anything while using ah-inspiring fresh herbs and spices. For me, my domain has become all things liquid: soups, sauces, drinks, dressings, and marinades. I don't think this would be true except for the necessity of making everything from scratch in Costa Rica.

It was on a flight home from Central America that next year that my dream career and I finally met. I had picked up a Natural Health magazine in the Houston airport for some light reading on my final leg back to Salt Lake. It was there that I read an advertisement for a school of naturopathic medicine. The ad literally read, "You will be a naturopathic physician." Still having no idea what the heck that was, I jumped on Google as soon as I got home. An hour later I knew it was a match made in heaven.

The first thing I found was a description of the tenets of naturopathic philosophy, and they read like a page from my own journal. The first tenet, which is the bedrock on which all else stands, is that innate in the wisdom of nature is the power to heal. Nature is wise, does not make mistakes, and can always return to health given the required circumstances. This I understood from a lifelong struggle with my own health. I was born with asthma, got colds and bronchitis easily, and had many rounds of pneumonia and strep throat. It was from those experiences that I knew I could prevent an asthma attack if I ate well, slept enough, and generally took care of myself. Asthma attacks and illness were not a given for me. Their occurrence was based on circumstance, and I knew even as a child the circumstances that promoted health over disease.

The second tenet is to do no harm. This is a universal truth in all healing modalities, and yet I have since learned naturopathic medicine take this to the deepest level, using medicine of the least force first before overpowering the body with drugs and surgery. While drugs and surgery are sometimes required, there is much that can be done to prevent their necessity. The naturopathic tools, particularly whole food, clean water, hydrotherapy, herbs and homeopathy, work to ignite the body's own healing mechanism to restore balance without need of more forceful intervention.

The third tenet is to treat the whole person; body, mind, and spirit. Again, having a lifetime of illness to experiment with, I knew my mental, emotional, and spiritual well-being had as much influence on my physical health as anything. I was so excited to be reading this I could hardly sit still. I read on.

Number four, to find and treat the root cause. In all my years in and out of doctors' offices, not once had there been a discussion of why I had asthma in the first place, where it came from, what its cause was, let alone how to treat that. In somewhat different terms, here was my lifelong quest for deeper understanding. To get to the root of an issue is as much what drives me in life as anything. I now knew why I

had spent five years getting a chemistry degree.

Number five fell right in with number one, prevention is the best medicine. I had so much experience with the difference between preventing my asthma by way of my daily choices versus going through the painful, difficult, and flat-out scary reality of having an asthma attack. This was not rocket science. This was simple, common sense, and yet I had never seen it written so succinctly.

Then the last tenet, like the final pieces of a puzzle, made everything clear. Doctor as teacher. Yes, that is who I am.

Eight months later I was sitting at orientation in Portland, Oregon, at the National College of Naturopathic Medicine, embarking on a four-year journey of exploration into the human body, nature's laws, and myself. It was on that first day that I met Tanda Cook, and like we used to do in elementary school, we became best friends immediately. Never did we dream that we would end up in Bozeman, Montana, running a clinic together and writing this cookbook. Yet here we are, and I couldn't be happier or more grateful.

Dr. Sarah Marshall, ND,
Bozeman, Montana
July 2011

PART II

"The phenomenon of health is a living activity, not a product. It is not something to have, but a way to be." - Robert Hoke

WHAT IS HEALTH?

As a society, we talk about "health" all the time, but do we really know what "health" is? Can we define it? How do we know when we have it?

When we ask our patients this question, we often get responses like "to not feel pain" or "to not get sick." We want you to think about this a minute and write down your definition of health. We challenge you to try to think of your own definition in the positive voice. Write what health is to you, as opposed to what it is not. Yes, we want you to take a minute to write down your definition in the pages of this book right now. It's that important. Go ahead. Go get a pen. We are serious. Yes, right now. Don't worry, we'll wait.

My definition of health:

_____

_____

_____

_____

We define health with two words: balance and freedom. Balance is a law of nature. To have any system in nature work properly, it must have balance in that system. With our personal health, this means there must be balance between our internal physical systems and all the systems in our lives, including work, family, and play. Freedom is the result of good health. In our practices, most of our patients are motivated to achieve health because of their pain and discomfort. If we don't feel well, we will do just about anything to feel better. However, what happens to our motivation once we feel better? Once the headaches are gone, the sugar cravings have disappeared, we have tons of energy, and can sleep through the night what motivates us to continue making choices every day to remain healthy?

Freedom. We want energy so we can play with our kids and grandkids. We want a good night's sleep so we can perform better at work, make more money, go on more vacations. We want to be strong and fit so we can run a marathon, play on a baseball team, or go on a mountain bike ride and enjoy the summer sun. Freedom is what our health can give us. Freedom to do whatever we dream of doing without our body standing in our way
The next natural question is, how do we do that? How do we balance our lives and our

HOW DO WE ACHIEVE
BALANCE AND FREEDOM IN OUR LIFE AND OUR BODY?

bodies? The answer is to add health. By adding health and not just fighting disease, you can bring your whole life into balance. Health and disease operate in our body just like light and darkness operate in the world around us. I have another question for you to answer. How do you light a dark room? If you walk into a dark room, what do you do?

Right, turn on the light. OK, what if it doesn't work, what else could you do? Light a candle, open the blinds, tear the roof off. Yes! These are all examples of how to add light to the room. There are two things in this analogy I want you to consider. I have asked this question to thousands of people, and not once has anyone suggested we cut the darkness out. So far we have not invented a machine we can hook up to the window and use to remove the darkness or a chemical that will dissolve it away and leave light behind. It isn't possible. That's because darkness isn't a physical thing— darkness is the absence of a physical thing. Darkness is simply the absence of light.

Disease, like darkness, is not actually a thing, it is the absence of a thing—it's the absence of health. Disease results from the lack of healing. Anywhere in the body where there is the presence of disease, there is also a lack of the healing process. What we call disease, the physical changes to the body that result from imbalances, is actually the body's best attempt to compensate for the current circumstances—its adaptive physiology. The body does not make mistakes. Everything it is doing—weight gain, pain, hormone imbalance, or even cancer—it does for a very specific reason: to cause the least harm to itself based on the conditions it is in. The body always has the innate ability to return to health as long as the necessary conditions to do so are available. To truly heal or prevent disease, you must add health. If we focus on adding health and supporting that healing process, the body will return to

the balanced state we call health and the result us the freedom to do anything you choose with your life.

How do we Add Health?

I want you to answer this one for yourself. Write down what adds health to your life. Nope, we still aren't kidding. Go for it. Right now.

What adds health to my life:

_____

_____

_____

The usual responses we get to this question when we ask our patients are: eat a healthy diet, exercise, drink enough water, have fun, maintain healthy relationships, etc. Those are exactly right. In essence, these are the things that make up the activities of our daily life, the choices we make every day, and we break them down into seven categories:

1. The foods we eat (or diet)
2. How we move (or exercise)
3. How we breathe
4. What we drink
5. How we sleep
6. How we eliminate (or detoxify both physically and emotionally)
7. How we play, work and enjoy life with those we love

The choices we make in each of these categories will either add health to our lives or lead to disease.

The Food We Eat

It's not an accident that the number one item on our list is food. So much health can be added via this area that we love and specialize in. With this book you will learn how to add health through the foods you eat by choosing whole, gluten-free, dairy-free foods every day. That being said, food is more than simply a fuel source, as we tell our patients. We do need food, and what we put in our mouth matters. And we understand that food is so much more than just nutrition. Food is celebration. Food is comfort. For some of us food is love. We coach people on the importance of intuitive eating and mindfulness about why they eat.

We ask our patients, and you, to respect the diverse ways food can add to the quality of your lives. Just because there is gluten in the birthday cake does not mean you can't eat it. It becomes about learning to listen to the signals your body is giving you, i.e., your symptoms, when you eat certain foods. You and your body can easily discover how to eat foods that truly make you feel great while living a life full of celebration, freedom, balance, love, community, and joy…or, in other words, a life of health.

How We Move

You can add health to your life by moving your body every day. We don't use the word "exercise," as it usually gives many of us the notion of having to join a gym or train for a marathon, which, for many of us, doesn't motivate at all. Instead, simply think of moving yourself in your favorite way. This is a category where you can really get two for one—if you move and play! Dance, jump, run, skip, do yoga, throw a ball, go for a swim. Play on the playground with your kids. Take a garden walk. If running is your thing, go nuts, but if not, find out what really makes your heart race…and sing!

How We Breathe

Breathing is the most important of all the lifestyle categories. Not one of us would last long without breathing. Yet, how many of us do this consciously? In our practice, we recommend that every patient take one hundred conscious breaths a day. This adds health in several ways. First, it brings us into the present moment to just be, where we are, for a minute or two. Second, it has long been proven that taking slow, deep breaths can decrease anxiety, lower blood pressure, and enhance brain function. Lastly, stress is a known cause of many disease states, and simply taking a few deep, conscious breaths when we are angry, frustrated, tired, or annoyed can greatly enhance our well-being and add health to our life.

What We Drink

Our body is made up of 60–80 percent water, depending upon our age (more as an infant and less as we get older). Chronic dehydration is a major issue in our culture and contributes to so many disease states it is impossible to list them all. If we are thirsty, we are already dehydrated. Water provides the medium in which all of our physiologic processes take place. Water is the river in our body that carries oxygen and nutrition to our cells and removes wastes and toxins from them. To not drink enough water every day is like washing your dishes in the same sink water for weeks at a time.

How much is enough? The gold standard we use in our practice is the number equivalent to one half of your body weight (in pounds) in ounces. For a 150-pound person, that would be equivalent to 75 ounces (or about 2 quarts) of water every day. This number should be increased if you do rigorous exercise, especially in a dry or hot climate. Additionally, if you consume caffeine or alcohol, an equal volume of water should be added for the amount you drink. For example, 12 ounces of water should be added to your daily total for every 12 ounces of coffee consumed.

How We Sleep

The only part of our body that sleeps is our brain. When we sleep, our internal organs get very active and busy regenerating and repairing any damage that has occurred during the day. During sleep, our brain processes and integrates information together. We recommend each of our patients get seven to eight hours of sleep every night. We also recommend everyone sleep in total darkness and go to bed and wake up at the same time every day. This routine helps solidify a strong circadian rhythm and supports hormone balance, cortisol levels, and our repair hormone, human growth hormone. This results in better memory, concentration, stable mood, higher day time energy, efficient weight loss, and even contributes to cancer prevention.

How We Work, Play and Enjoy Life with Those We Love

Having fun is essential in life and to health. Happiness and joy are, absolutely, some of the most powerful ways to heal the body. All too often, we lose the ability to play as we grow up and don't think we have time because of work and family responsibilities. We become resigned to the idea that work must be hard and life difficult to prove their value. The old adage 'if your love what you do, you will never work a day in your life' couldn't be more true or more preventative of disease. Additionally, committing to having fun with the people in your life can do amazing things for the health of your body and your relationships.

We often have to help our patients remember what it is they love to do, and to remember we can play through our whole day by changing our attitude about our work and home lives. We want you to take this moment right now and write down at least five things you love to do, and at least three of them should be things you can do every day, rain or shine. If they are all things you feel you cannot do, or haven't done for a long time, notice what is standing in your way. Time? Location?

Money? Availability? Make a commitment to create the possibility of more of these in your life. Get creative.

What I love to do:

1.

2.

3.

4.

5.

How We Eliminate

The last category is one that, as a culture, we often overlook. We often focus our attention only on what we put into our body and not on what we let go of. Physiologic detoxification is a hugely important process that our body requires to maintain health. There are many, many health systems available to support detoxification and elimination. Eating a whole foods diet supports this process by providing your body with the vitamins and minerals it needs as co-factors to the many enzymes which detoxify the body. Additionally, antioxidants, primarily found in fruits and vegetables, are essential co-factors for our ability to detoxify the body. Lastly, the fiber in vegetables and fruits supports digestive health and elimination as well.

Emotional elimination is another topic we talk to our patients about and a key way to add health to our lives. We often see people holding back, not saying what they really think, or being stressed out and not having a healthy outlet for it. We often ask what people do to relieve stress, and more often than not they don't have an answer. It's hard to have physical well-being without having emotional well-being. And food often plays a role in both.

EATING WHOLE FOODS

Foods that grow are whole foods. These foods come to our plate in the same condition, or nearly the same condition, as they are found growing in nature. Whole foods, foods that grow, are the best at growing healthy people. The U.S. Department of Agriculture defines whole foods as foods that are "unprocessed or unrefined, or as unprocessed and unrefined as possible." That addition of "as possible" really adds considerable legal gray area; it essentially leaves the door open for processed foods, unfortunately, to advertise that they are more natural and healthy than they really are. A more exact definition of a whole food is anything that a caveman would recognize as food. Tanda has been quoted as defining whole foods as "any food that can be picked from a tree, plucked from the ground, or shot." We are from Montana, after all.

> " *If we eat whole food, we consume the food and nutrients as Mother Nature intended, in its most complete, and absorbable way.* "

What is so great about whole foods?

The importance of eating whole foods has to do with the completeness of the food, as well as the state of the nutrients in it. A whole food contains everything neccessary, including enzymes, macronutrients, micronutrients, and fiber for you to eat, digest, and absorb as nature intended. Whenever we process a food by grinding, rolling, milling, canning, cooking, heating, pasteurizing, baking, roasting, smoking, steaming, etc., we degrade the nutrition inside. Processing a food begins the breakdown of nutrients, which is why processed foods contain so many preservatives and undergo unnatural preservative techniques. The goal of most processing is to increase food's shelf life, which is nearly always contrary to health. The reason companies fortify their flours, breads, and cereals is to try to put back what they took out, which they will never be able to completely accomplish. If we eat whole food, we consume the food and nutrients as Mother Nature intended, in its most available, complete, and absorbable way.

What is wrong with eating processed foods?

Mother Nature grows her foods in such a way as to maximize their longevity as long as you don't crack them open. As soon as you slice an apple or mill a seed into flour, you have exposed the vitamins, minerals, and enzymes on the inside to the air. In the air is oxygen, and once the food is exposed to oxygen, a process of decay, called oxidation, begins to set in, destroying it.

The way processing gets around this problem is primarily through adding chemicals (preservatives) that slow the process of decay. The issue with processed foods becomes twofold; one, they have less nutrition because they have been degraded, and two, they have added chemicals that ultimately contribute to disease. The other major concern is that many processed foods have significant amounts of added salt, sugar, and unhealthy fats that also contribute to our most common disease processes, including obesity, cancer, heart disease, and diabetes.

Isn't cooking food at home also processing it?

Yes, by definition it is. As naturopathic doctors we always recommend getting a significant portion of your calories from raw foods, more in the summer months and less in the winter. However, when you do cook your foods you are greatly increasing the number of vital nutrients you are absorbing into your body if you bring your foods home in their whole state and mostly prepare your meals from scratch (as this cookbook will help you to do). Processed foods, on the other hand, are usually processed and cooked months before they are eaten.

But whole foods go bad so fast!

It is actually good news that whole food goes bad. Food that lasts forever isn't food; it is a chemically produced food-like substance designed for longevity over nutrition. Food that can go bad (or has a short shelf life) is still alive and has the highest nutrient content, which gives our bodies essential, vital energy. In the United States, one of the proven causes of our obesity epidemic, as well as the rise in heart disease, cancer, and diabetes, is eating a calorie-rich, nutrient poor processed food diet. Conversely, eating a diet of whole foods provides nutrient-dense calories that add health to your life. The idea is to eat them often so they don't have time to go bad. We could have named this book "Food That Rots," but it doesn't quite have the same ring to it.

Here are a few truths to dispel some common myths we encounter in our grocery stores.

Myth: Foods made with whole grains count as a whole food.

Truth: There are many products out there that advertise they are "made with" whole ingredients, which can be confusing. While processing from whole ingredients is a step in the right direction away from nutrient-void white flour, any bread, cereal, or baked good is still processed, no matter how you slice it.

Myth: Foods labeled 'made with all natural ingredients' are always healthy.

Truth: The label "natural" has not been clearly defined, nor its use in advertising well regulated. What this means, unfortunately, is that the word "natural" on a box doesn't really mean much. The good news is you can get around all this by simply eating whole foods, as they are always "made with all natural ingredients".

Myth: Organic food is the same thing as whole food.

Truth: Whole foods are not always organic, and what is labeled "organic" is not always whole. As the organic food industry has grown, there have been millions of new organic processed foods that, because of advertising, people feel are healthy choices. We hate to break it to you, but an organic gummy bear is still a gummy bear, nonetheless. If you are going to eat gummy bears anyway, organic is probably a better choice, but if you're interested in adding health, we'd recommend a strawberry instead.

Myth: Fruit juice is good for you.

Truth: Fruit juice is essentially sugar water with a tiny bit of vitamins and minerals, some of which are added at the factory. It takes between eight and sixteen oranges to make one glass of juice. Translation: for every glass of juice you drink, you consume at least eight (if not sixteen) times more sugar than you would by consuming the whole fruit. The detrimental effects of the sugar in juice far outweigh the claimed health benefits, not to mention that you lose the beneficial fiber as well. Fruit, on the other hand, is very good for you and should be eaten in its whole form.

A note about added sugar: Juice companies often claim a healthier product by declaring "no sugar added." While this is an improvement over juices that have been sweetened artificially, this debate is like trying to say a bowl of ice cream is significantly healthier than a bowl of ice cream with chocolate sauce on top. In the end, it's all sugar, and the only difference is how much.

Myth: If you are going to buy processed food, low fat is the best option.

Truth: Fat is what makes most foods other than fruits and vegetables taste good. We have often said it is the "saturated" fats that make food "satisfying." If you remove the fat from processed food, it tastes like cardboard. The processed food industry is well aware of this, so they add salt, a lot of salt, to make it taste better, but then it is too salty, so they add sugar to balance the salt. Additionally, fat is one of the key ways our body knows we have eaten enough and tells us to stop. Consequently, we actually eat more of a low fat food. When choosing to eat boxed, canned, or otherwise processed food, always go for the full-fat option.

Myth: Eating whole foods means eating "the whole food," including the roots, stems, seeds, and all.

Truth: Eating whole foods means eating the whole, edible portions of the food. When you eat whole foods, you are still allowed to manicure your fruits and meats and veggies; you can wash, peel, chop, julienne, and dice to your heart's content. Eating whole foods still means that you can trim the woody stem and squiggly rootlets from your beautiful beets, although you should save the greens because they are really tasty, too. You don't have to eat the "bad spots" or the banana peel. It's not necessary to eat the apple core, seeds and all (unless you want to).

WHAT ARE THE HEALTHY FOODS TO EAT?

An overwhelming amount of chronic disease has its causal roots in what we choose to put in our bodies. Until very recently in human history, what to eat was not commonly in question. Each generation ate what the generation before them had always eaten, and health generally prevailed. We live in a unique time where we look to scientists and government instead of our grandmothers to instruct us on the most beneficial nutrients to supply our bodies with sustenance. As it turns out, even with all the food science and technological development today many chronic diseases are on the rise. Mother Nature still knows how to make the best food. The following information is to give you a better understanding of why eating a whole food, gluten-free, dairy-free diet is the best choice to add health to your life. These recommendations are simply guidelines to add health to your life and not to be confused with laws, rules, or dogma. The food you eat every day is your choice. The question becomes: what is the result you desire from eating food? If you desire health, then the closer you choose to follow our recommendations, the healthier you will become.

In nature, health is the default state. If you are experiencing symptoms or disease in your life, you need to change the circumstances you are creating for your body to get a new result. Diet is not about right and wrong or good and bad. There are not "good foods" and "bad foods." What there are, are foods that work to produce health and foods that do not. Health results when the foods you put into your body provide it with the right information, which results in health. Disease results when the foods you choose to put in your body work against your body's desire to be healthy. Health is

our body's natural state. Choose foods that add health and balance and your body will thank you.

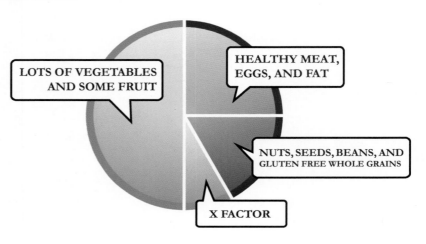

The Whole Food Plate

We have slightly modified the new 2001 U.S. Department of Agriculture "My Plate" to reflect our views of an even healthier, balanced diet. The majority of your diet should be vegetables, eaten at every meal, and some fruit, eaten mostly between meals as a snack. The next greatest portion, calorically, should be healthy meats and fats, followed by a limited amount of whole, gluten-free grains, nuts, and seeds used more as condiments or snacks in your diet. Finally we included the X factor, which is when "life happens". This is the family dinner when lasagna and bread are served, a pot luck topped off with ice cream sundaes, or a run in with an artisan bakery while traveling. The food you choose to eat should not be about strict rules or dogma. Life, and the food in it, should be enjoyed in the best way possible to add health. Sarah has often been quoted saying, "life is too short to not eat crème Brulee". Food and diet should not be about depravity. Food is so much more than just calories and fuel, and it should be so. Food is community! Food is celebration!

What is healthy protein?

In our experience, the healthiest protein comes from animals, fish, and fowl. Our body is designed to eat meat. Although there are many modern reasons people chose to be vegetarian, it is our expert opinion that physiologically, the most bioavailable protein is found in meat and eggs. If vegetarianism is your choice for the foods you eat simply replace the meat section of the whole food plate with ample legumes, nuts and gluten-free grains to ensure sufficient protein.

It absolutely matters where your meat and eggs come from. Healthy meat is raised on its own natural diet. That means grass-fed cows, wild game, wild-caught fish, and poultry and eggs from pasture-raised chickens. For more information on these animals and where to buy products made from them in your area, visit www.eatwild.com and www.localharvest.com.

What is a healthy fat?

Fats from healthy, happy animal sources such as those found in pork, beef, poultry, game, fish, seafood, and organic butter, organic olive oil, and organic coconut oil are the best choices. These foods contain moderate to high levels of "satisfying" saturated fats and essential fatty acids such as omega-3s, and are the easiest to digest, absorb and use by the body.

As in protein, where you get your fat matters. Due to modern farming and ranching practices, organic grass-fed sources are an absolute must when it comes to choosing healthy animal fat sources. More and more grocers are carrying these products, and a quick Internet search for grass-fed animals in your area should provide a wealth of information. For more information on these animals and where to buy them in your area, visit www.eatwild.com and www.localharvest.com. When buying olive oil and coconut oil, buy organic, cold-pressed or expeller-pressed oils. The best butter is organic pasture raised (see resources page 200)

What is a healthy carbohydrate?

Many people misunderstand and believe that a predominantly meat and vegetable diet is high in protein and low in carbohydrates. Fruits and vegetables are carbohydrates. Referring to our whole food plate, you can see that vegetables and fruits are meant to make up the majority of our dietary calories. This means consuming as many as six to nine cups of fresh veggies a day. That is plenty of carbohydrates to successfully and · healthfully maintain the body.

So what makes these carbohydrates healthier? Fruits and veggies are complex carbohydrates, another way to call them whole foods. If you eat the whole grain as it was grown in nature, or the whole vegetable, you are consuming carbohydrates they way humans have been consuming them for thousands of years. This provides our body not only with carbohydrates, but with soluble and insoluble fiber, essential vitamins and minerals, and loads of antioxidants. When we eat complex carbohydrates combined with healthy fats and protein, our blood sugar increases slowly and remains steady for a long time. When we consume simple, sugar-filled carbohydrates, it is like throwing paper on a fire. We get a hot, quick burn followed by a steep crash in blood sugar, which causes a craving for more sugar, which feeds the cycle.

Simple carbohydrates come in the form of sugar, corn syrup, agave, maple syrup, honey, white rice, white potatoes, and anything made with flour (i.e., processed grains: baked goods, pastries, breads, pasta, cookies, crackers, food bars, etc.). One of the primary influences on the rise of chronic disease has been the replacement of calories from fats by calories from simple carbohydrates. Humans have been eating approximately two thousand calories (or more) a day for generation upon generation. When we began reducing the number of calories of fat we were consuming in the 1970s, we didn't reduce the overall calories we consumed; we simply ate more sugar, an ever-increasing amount of sugar. In the early 1900s, the average American consumed 25 pounds of sugar per year; today Americans consume 156 pounds of sugar per person per year.

WHAT ABOUT FOOD ALLERGIES AND INTOLERANCES?

For many of our patients the world of food allergies and intolerances has become riddled with misinformation and confusion. We will attempt to clarify a few things here; however, a detailed discussion about foodrelated diseases, intolerances, addictions, allergies, and sensitivities is beyond the scope of this book. At the end of the day, the prescription is the same—avoid the foods your body doesn't like, the foods that cause symptoms and disease. For the sake of ease and simplicity, in this book we will use the word "intolerance" to refer to all adverse food reactions.

To clarify, a food allergy specifically excites an immunemodulated response in the body which can easily be tested for (these are specific antibodies your immune system produces as a reaction to a specific food. More information regarding testing below). However, there are many other ways that a problematic food can cause symptoms and disease processes inside your body, many of which are poorly understood. This is usually described as a food intolerance or food sensitivity. Unfortunately words and terms to describe food sensitivities, intolerances and allergies are exchanged without much agreement or consistency of their definitions or meanings, even, and especially among the medical community.

Until recently, food intolerances eliciting no allergic response were dismissed and patients were told that they didn't have an issue with the suspected food, which we now know isn't true. Specific disease processes such as celiac disease, dermatitis herpetiformis (an extremely itchy rash made up of bumps and blisters), and silent inflammation are not food allergies but, nevertheless, are critical food intolerance issues.

On a practical and somewhat disappointing note, it is true that the food you usually crave the most is often your worst allergy. This has to do with an intricate system of how your body manages pain and trauma and the chemical properties of the food that can cause a neurotransmitter "high" after eating a food your body is hurt by. In naturopathic medical school we often were told to look for allergies where there is addiction. By definition we are addicted to anything we cannot quit.

One way to investigate if your body is having an adverse reaction to some of the foods you are eating is to do laboratory testing for it. The typical types of tests available are skin tests, blood tests, saliva tests, and stool tests. The most common tests today specifically look for food allergies. Tests range anywhere from the five most common allergenic foods (wheat/gluten, dairy, soy, corn, and eggs) to a more comprehensive two-hundred-foods panel; tests run between $75 and $200, respectively. Each type of test has its own limitations and advantages, but they all can begin to show you if you might need to experiment with avoiding certain foods.

One issue with this type of testing is that it is common for someone to test negative for a food allergy that is still causing a problem in their body which is why the true gold-standard test for food allergies and intolerances is to do an elimination challenge.

The elimination challenge

Essentially the best way to know how a food is affecting you is to stop eating it. Then add it back into your diet after some time and note the changes. Some people notice a difference in how they feel in a matter of days after eliminating a food. Some don't notice any changes until they add the food back in, when their old symptoms return and they realize how good they really felt without that food.

Elimination diets can range from simply the avoidance of one food for a few weeks all the way to eating only lamb and plain white rice for six weeks and slowly adding foods back into the diet one at a time over the course of several more weeks. In our practice we recommend all of our patients eliminate gluten and dairy products for a minimum of one month. We usually don't need to tell people to challenge their body by adding the food back in, because they usually experiment on their own and tell us how awful they felt after they indulged in pizza or ice cream. For best results, at the end of the month you should add one eliminated food back in at time and note any changes in how you feel.

Here is what we recommend:

Avoid all grains containing gluten (see gluten section for more information page 22), all dairy products (except butter), sugar, processed food, and alcohol for one month, and follow our Top Ten Diet Guidelines (page 30). Although sugar and alcohol are not typically food allergens, they are both highly inflammatory and can exacerbate reactions to other foods in the body.

Some of our patients find it very helpful to keep a foodmood journal during the challenge. Keep track of what you eat and how you feel every day during your challenge, and continue to note how you feel after consuming any of the eliminated foods. Be sure to notice your energy levels, quality of sleep, appetite, digestion, mood and irritability levels, ability to concentrate and remember things, how your period goes, your skin, and how your body feels physically in your muscles and joints. Food intolerances often affect our digestion, but they can affect virtually any system in the body, including our brain, mood, and emotional state. (See more on the specific effects of gluten and dairy on pages 22 & 26)

If you want to take your challenge a step further, we recommend you eliminate corn, eggs, and soy as well. We find that about 10 percent of our population has adverse reactions to these foods, where nearly all of our patients find gluten and dairy to negatively affect their health. (See our resources section on page 200 for more info on finding blood tests for food allergies.)

Remember to be gentle with yourself. The process of investigating food intolerances can often be emotionally challenging. We do not eat food simply for nutritional sustenance. Food is, and has always been, intricately interwoven into our relationships with ourselves and our world. Food is often about reward, loss, celebration, community, connection, and love. Honor and acknowledge what you are feeding with food, and let this journey of exploration into health open the door to unleashed self-expression, true joy, freedom, balance, and love in all aspects of your life.

THE GLUTEN ISSUE

What is gluten?

Gluten is a protein found in wheat, rye, triticale, and barley. Its name comes from the root word "glue," because it is what gives bread and other grain-based foods their sticky, stretchy, gluey nature.

These grains are touted for their relatively high protein content. Relative to what, exactly? Relative to other plants. The most protein-rich foods are meat, fish, and poultry. The protein content, by weight, of cooked meat, fish, poultry, and milk solids is between 15 percent and 40 percent. The protein content of cooked grains, beans, lentils and peas ranges from 3 percent to 10 percent. Potatoes, fruits, and leafy green vegetables come in at 3 percent or lower.

The other issue beyond nutrient content is digestibility. We too often assume that just because there are certain nutrients in a food, it means we will be absorbing and utilizing all of them. It's not just what you eat, it is what you absorb and use. This is a key phrase we all should keep in the front of our minds when selecting foods at the grocery store. The digestibility of grains is an issue we will discuss further in a minute.

Why go gluten-free?

One of the issues with gluten is that it causes immune reactions that result in inflammation. Inflammation occurs as a natural healing process of the body whenever there has been an injury. Inflammation allows for the immune system cells, which are big and bulky, to sneak from your circulation into the surrounding tissues through holes in your arteries and intestinal walls and to get where the injury occurred. This process is essential to allow the immune system to heal an injury, but only for that short time. The issue with inflammation occurs when it happens chronically,

all the time, day in day out. In situations of chronic inflammation, the holes between cells are open all the time and not only does this allow immune cells into the intestines and stomach, but it also accidentally allows food partials out into the tissues where they don't belong. This describes a functional illness called "leaky gut" and is one of many theories of why gluten can be such an issue for people.

Leaky gut can leave us with these undigested food particles in all the wrong places, and they can quite literally gunk up the works of our bodies, causing an endless list of possible symptoms, from hormone imbalances to memory and concentration issues to additional food allergies, hay fever, and more severe diseases, such as autoimmune disease, osteoporosis, and neurologic disorders.

Lastly, our stressed-out, toxin-filled lives add to the issue. If our body is like a bath tub and we only have so much room for stressful events and substances, it is reasonable to see how we have decreased our internal resistance to gluten by increasing our stress levels with how much we try to do every day, eating processed, nutrient-deficient foods, and not taking proper care of our bodies.

We believe that health is about generating balance in our lives, and thus, as we decrease the stress in one department of our lives, that might give us more resilience in another. To be sure, we have found that smart food choices are a far easier way to decrease stress than getting our patients to work less or quit their draining jobs. Choosing a gluten-free lifestyle is a great way to add health to your life and decrease the overall stress your body has to process.

Gluten sensitivity vs. Celiac disease

Research suggests that about one in 133, or about 2.1 million people, have celiac disease, which is an autoimmune disease that literally allows gluten to lay siege to the small intestine. Furthermore, the research suggests an additional one person in seven is intolerant to gluten. Still more choose to remove gluten from their diets without any sort of diagnosis, as a means to a healthier lifestyle. In our personal practice, we have found more often than not that the removal of gluten from the diet of our patients dramatically improves their health. To wrap our head around this issue, we first need to get a little technical and define the difference between celiac disease and what is now being called non-celiac gluten sensitivity.

Celiac disease is an autoimmune disorder of the digestive tract that can occur in people of any age. It results in damage to the small intestine and interferes with the absorption of nutrients. People who have celiac disease suffer from issues of malabsorption and have an abnormal immune reaction to gluten. You can test for celiac disease by measuring if you have the autoantibody to your own intestinal cells.

We want to reiterate that celiac disease is an autoimmune disease, not a food allergy. The symptoms are triggered by eating foods that contain gluten, but gluten is not the cause of the disease.

Non-celiac gluten sensitivity is defined as an immunologic response to gluten (i.e., your immune system forms antibodies to gluten because it thinks that gluten is a foreign invader of the body and not a healthy food). There is no autoimmune response to the body in these cases. You can test for non-celiac gluten sensitivity by seeing if you have anti-gluten antibodies.
There is another class of people who have tested negative for both of the above but still feel better when they remove gluten from their diets. So far the research has not figured out this group of people, but clinically we, as naturopaths, see this frequently.

Thus the gold standard to determine if you are gluten sensitive is to remove gluten completely from your diet for thirty to ninety days and see how you feel (see section of how to do an elimination challenge). Most patients begin to notice a difference in their health in as little as one week. Some notice the greatest change when they add it back into their diet and symptoms they didn't even notice before return.

Haven't we been eating gluten and wheat for generations?

Yes, we have, but not as many generations as you would think. There are many theories out there for why we are "suddenly" having a problem with gluten. Some say it is due to the issues with the weakening of our immune systems as a result of living too clean a lifestyle; some say it is the result of genetic modification of our food; some say it is an issue of how we are processing foods and that if we ate the grains our ancestors ate, we would be fine. Truth is, we don't exactly know; the study of this issue is fairly new and the research is just getting under way.

We do want to share some interesting facts about the nature of grains themselves and evolution, and let you make your own decisions.

When were grains introduced into the human diet?

Our human ancestors have been eating grains containing gluten for between two thousand and ten thousand years, depending on our area of origin in the world. About ten thousand years ago, people in the Far East began to cultivate many grains for consumption, not just wheat. Before this, people foraged for fruits and nuts, and got most of their protein from hunting animals. Grains were not a viable source of nutrition for several reasons. Grains were hard to find because the grasses were relatively sparse compared with how we cultivate today. Grain seeds were much smaller than the modified versions we know now. Lastly, grains are practically inedible and potentially poisonous when uncooked, and therefore were not an appreciable source of calories for our ancestors.

What are grains? Grains are seeds. What do seeds "want" to do in nature? They "want" to be eaten, moved away from the parent plant in the stomach of a bird or animal, and then leave the body of that animal undigested so that they can grow into another plant. These seeds or grains, including wheat, have many natural defense mechanisms trying very hard to not be easily digestible, and some of these defenses remain even after being cooked.

One of the issues with those ancient grains that still exists today is the part about being inedible. The only way to consume grains is to cook them, and if you have ever made brown rice, you know to cook it for a long time. This process breaks down the exterior of the seed and allows our digestive tract to access the nutrition inside. However, we still cannot absorb all of what is in a grain.

Who should consider avoiding gluten?

Truth be told, in our practice, we have all of our patients remove gluten (ideally thirty to ninety days) to see how they feel off it and how they feel when they add it back in. Because one of the results of a gluten sensitivity is malabsorption of your nutrition, symptoms of gluten intolerance can literally affect [or] show up in in any system of the body from head to toe. There are some specific symptoms and diseases that are commonly associated with a gluten issue.

The most common diseases affiliated with gluten issues are:

- Anemia
- Depression
- Anxiety
- Seizures
- Attention Deficit Disorder or Attention Deficit Hyperactivity Disorder
- Learning disabilities
- Arthritis

- Autoimmune disease
- Hypothyroidism
- Osteoporosis or osteopenia
- Infertility or miscarriage(s)
- Migraines
- Canker sores in the mouth
- Irritable Bowel Syndrome or Inflammatory Bowel Disorder
- Crohn's disease
- Ulcerative colitis
- Raynaud's phenomenon

Frequently, people who are gluten intolerant complain of diarrhea, constipation, and stomach cramps. Skin irritations are also common and may include hives, acne, and flaky, scratchy skin. Many people report fatigue, achiness, weight loss or inability to lose weight, moodiness, and inability to concentrate. When a patient is diagnosed with a laundry list of food allergies; gluten is often a keystone food to the overall issue.

We have also seen gluten intolerances correlate to:

- Numbness of the hands and feet
- Premenstrual Syndrome and menstrual irregularities
- Adrenal fatigue
- Hormonal imbalance
- Hypoglycemia
- Headaches
- Chronic pain anywhere
- Acid reflux and other gastrointestinal disturbances such as chronic constipation or diarrhea

Also, we want to highlight some common issues seen in kiddos who are sensitive to gluten.

- Acid reflux and Gastroesophageal Reflux Disease
- Chronically spitting up
- Failure to thrive, or other nutritional deficiencies
- Chronic diaper rash
- Frequent colds, flu, and ear infections

- Bed wetting
- Diarrhea/constipation
- Unexplained irritability, fussiness, and mood or behavior disorders
- Other food allergies

What foods likely contain gluten?

- Baked goods, pastries, cookies, cakes, scones
- Pasta
- Bagels
- Pretzels
- Crackers
- Pizza
- Beer
- Soy sauce
  Hidden sources can be found in:
- Processed meats
- Salad dressings, condiments
- Candy
- Soup
- Gravy
- Vitamin supplements
- Personal care products

What about oats?

Oats are genetically gluten free; however, the processing of wheat and oats has been so married together that there is often cross contamination between the growing, transportation, processing, and packaging of oats such that they cannot always be labeled a gluten-free food. If you or someone you know has a moderate to severe gluten sensitivity, only GF-labeled oats should be consumed.

Gluten-free grains:

The most commonly found gluten-free grains are corn, rice, quinoa, amaranth, teff, buckwheat, millet, sorghum, and wild rice. There are several other foods used to make gluten-free flours, including potatoes, garbanzo beans, almonds, and even coconut. Today's marketplace is full of gluten-free options. Keep in mind these are all processed foods and should be limited in their consumption to promote the most health possible in your diet. See our resources section for more information on our favorite gluten-free products.

THE DAIRY ISSUE

Like gluten, pasteurized dairy (versus raw dairy) is an inflammatory food. Many people are already aware of lactose intolerance, which is one aspect of the problems with dairy, but it is not the entire issue. Lactose is a sugar found in milk. Many people do not have the enzymes to digest lactose, which can cause stomach upset, gas, bloating, nausea, and even vomiting when people with this intolerance ingest dairy.

Along with lactose intolerance, many people also have an intolerance to casein, a protein found in dairy, and they experience similar digestive symptoms along with many other signs of inflammation in their body when they eat dairy. One of the most common places we see dairy intolerance symptoms is in the respiratory system. Chronic sinusitis, ear infections, pharyngitis, strep throat, sore throats, tonsillitis, breathing problems, snoring, postnasal drip, asthma, bronchitis, and any lung ailment can also be symptoms of a dairy intolerance. We have also found that acne, particularly on the face, is frequently correlated with a dairy allergy or sensitivity.

Who should consider avoiding dairy?

The scientific research has proven that 50 percent of the U.S. population is intolerant to dairy due to lactose intolerance, which is considerably lower than what we see in our clinical practice. Nearly all African Americans, Asian Americans, and Mexican Americans are lactose intolerant. The percentages go down measurable for North American Caucasians; however, lactose is not the only issue with milk.

Dairy allergy vs. lactose intolerance

A dairy allergy is an immune reaction that results in inflammation and tissue damage. Such a response to food can be exhibited in any part of the body; therefore, it can cause a wide range of problems. Food allergies also interfere with nutrient absorption, resulting in conditions such as iron deficiency or anemia, osteoporosis, and fatigue. Lactose intolerance is an enzyme deficiency, not an allergy. However, lactose intolerance can be the result of a dairy allergy, and the two are frequently confused.

What dairy does in the body

Allergies cause a chronic state of inflammation in the body, damage tissues, and decrease the optimal functioning of any system in the body. Specifically, we want to highlight some of the most common red flags of dairy sensitivity. Dairy often causes an overproduction of mucus in the body. In any condition where there is chronic nasal swelling, runny nose, or excess mucus, like asthma and even cystic fibrosis, dairy should be avoided. In children, chronic ear infections are one of the most common symptoms of a dairy sensitivity. In adults we can hear a dairy allergy in how someone sounds when they talk. Anyone who sounds stuffed up all the time or speaks with a nasally voice should try eliminating dairy and see if this clears up.

Lactose intolerance often causes:

- Gas
- Bloating
- Diarrhea
- Stomach pain and cramping

Additionally, disorders and diseases commonly associated with dairy are:

- Allergies and hay fever
- Asthma
- Frequent sinus infections

- Frequent colds and flus
- Post nasal drip
- Difficulty breathing through your nose
- Chronic stuffiness
- Sleep apnea
- Snoring
- Poor sleep quality

Many people also report fatigue, generalized achiness, difficulty maintaining a healthy weight, moodiness and inability to concentrate.

We have also seen dairy correlated to:

- Acid reflux
- Gluten allergies and other food allergies
- Acne
- Osteoporosis and osteopenia
- Arthritis
- Chronic pain

We want to highlight some common issues seen in kiddos who are sensitive to dairy.
Note: While lactose intolerance is quite rare in infants, dairy allergy or intolerance is not.
Common symptoms of a dairy intolerance in kids:
- Acid reflux and GERD
- Chronically spitting up
- Failure to thrive or other nutritional deficiencies
- Chronic diaper rash
- Bed wetting in children past the age of potty training
- Frequent colds, flus and ear infections
- Diarrhea/constipation
- Unexplained irritability, fussiness, and mood or behavior disorders

Diagnosed with a laundry list of food allergies, dairy, like gluten, can be keystone food to the issue.

Foods that are made from dairy:

- Milk
- Yogurt
- Cheese
- Sour cream
- Ice cream
- Butter

Note: Whey is derived from dairy, so if you are sensitive to dairy, you should not consume whey protein.

Hidden sources of dairy

Many food additives are derived from milk, and if you have a severe sensitivity or desire to truly eliminate all sources of cow dairy from your life, avoid any product containing milk solids, casein, sodium caseinate, caseinate, or lactose. Of course, if you eat whole foods versus processed foods, this won't be an issue.

Hidden sources of dairy:
- Processed meats
- Salad dressings, condiments
- Candy
- Vitamin supplements
- Personal care products
- Bakery glazes
- Breath mints
- Powdered creamers
- Fortified cereals
- Protein powders
- Ice cream
- Infant formulas
- Nutrition bars
- Whipped toppings
- Soy meat substitutes

What about butter? You guys say it's good for you, but isn't butter considered dairy?

Yes, butter is considered dairy and it does contain a small amount of milk protein which can be an issue for the highly sensitive or allergic person. That being said, organic pasture butter is also an incredible superfood full of brain-building short-chain fatty acids and essential fat-soluble vitamins like vitamins A, D, E, and K. It is rare that we have a patient who is so sensitive to dairy that he or she reacts to butter. If this is the case, you can consume clarified butter. Clarified butter is made by melting butter and removing the white milk solids and leaving the orangey-yellow colored oil; this is also called ghee and is popularly used in Indian cuisine.

Why are we so sensitive to dairy today?

So why all these allergies and intolerances? Are food allergies and intolerances really more prevalent now, or have we simply been ignoring food as a cause of disease until recently? The research community has not come to a conclusion about this yet. There was a dentist about one hundred years ago named Weston A. Price who was making significant headway in proving that the consumption of processed grains and processed dairy were a significant cause of disease. He studied numerous indigenous cultures all over the world and noted that the way they ate was the greatest predictor of their health as well as the health of their offspring. The research of Weston A. Price is fascinating, thorough, and detailed. Please look up the Weston A. Price Foundation for more information.

Some food for thought about dairy: We are the only species on the planet to drink milk after infancy, and the only species to drink the milk of another species. So, with the rest of nature as our guide, perhaps we shouldn't drink milk at all.

We do consume dairy, however, and we have been doing so for somewhere between five thousand and ten thousand years, depending on our heritage and when the domestication of animals began. One fact that is not debatable and could be a major factor in our modern issue with milk consumption is that the milk we drink today is nothing like the milk of even one hundred years ago due to modern farming practices and pasteurization.

Pasteurized milk has been heated to high temperatures for an extended period of time to ensure no pathological bacteria survive. Unfortunately, this process also degrades the immune complexes, denatures the protein, creates free-radical damage to the fats, and continues to cause rancidity every day after the pasteurization process, making pasteurized milk a much less nutritious and more inflammatory food than its raw counterpart.

Another issue with modern milk is that it is produced from cows raised in a factory setting, and on the wrong diet to support their health. (We know what happens to us when we eat the wrong diet.) Many of these cows are far below their optimal health. If you eat the meat or drink the milk of unhealthy animals, the results show up as disease in you. Pasteurization is essential for the modern milk industry because E. coli infection is rampant in corn-fed cows (versus grass-fed cows) and must be controlled to avoid food poisoning. Dairy cows fed their natural diet of grass, grazing freely in open-range conditions, do not carry these disease-causing pathogens, and pasteurization is not necessary because they give clean, healthy milk.

Some advocates of consuming raw milk say that the real issue with dairy is how the dairy cows are raised and how the milk is pasteurized, and that if we could only consume raw milk from cows raised on their native diet, as we did for the first 9,900 years of consuming dairy, we would have no issue with it. In our private practice, we still see people who have difficulty with well-made raw milk, which leads us to believe that there is more to the dairy issue.

If we don't eat dairy, how do we get calcium and vitamin D?

A significant reason for Americans' intense loyalty to dairy products is that we have all been lead to believe that dairy is the only significant source of calcium and vitamin D available. However, a significant amount of calcium is also found in dark green, leafy vegetables like spinach, kale, turnip greens, beet greens, broccoli, cabbage, brussels sprouts, etc. Two cups of spinach have the same amount of calcium as 8 ounces of whole milk. The main, and best, source of vitamin D is sun exposure. UV-B exposure on the skin generates the active form of vitamin D, vitamin D3. You can also get some (but not all) vitamin D from farm-fresh eggs, organic butter from grass-fed cows, fish, fish oil, and grass-fed meats.

There is something else operating here that makes the nutrient comparison between processed dairy and whole foods unfair. The processed foods are cheating. The most significant dietary sources of calcium in the American diet do come almost exclusively from processed food sources. Did you know that skim milk is a processed food? As we described earlier, a processed food is anything that is no longer in its natural raw state. The pasteurization of milk makes it a processed food, and that's not the only thing done to milk before it gets to your grocery store shelf.

First, all milk either remains "whole milk" or becomes skim milk. The 1 percent and 2 percent milks are made by adding back the fat that was taken out to make it skim milk. However, the fat has been heated and dried and then gets sprayed at extremely high pressure back into the skim milk to homogenize it and keep the water and fat from separating. Nutrients that are lost in the process, or were never there to begin with, are added. This is the meaning of the word "fortified."

Any food that has been "fortified" means the industry producing that food is adding in supplemental nutrients to increase the nutrient levels of that particular processed food item. Cereals are "fortified." Pastas are "fortified." Even orange juice is now fortified with calcium (there wasn't much in an orange to begin with). Most milk is also fortified with vitamin D and extra calcium. That means the milk you drink has added calcium and vitamin D in it bearing little resemblance to what was naturally there.

Why does fortification matter?

Why do we care whether or not a food is fortified? Fortification matters for the same reason processed food matters. Fortification is a deviation from the way Mother Nature intended your food to be, and the assumption is that we haven't done as good a job as she has. Additionally, many of the sources of the fortified nutrients are unpublicized and nearly impossible to track down. Some of the additives are biologically indigestible, and

our body can't absorb them no matter how much the industry has added to the food. This aspect of the food industry is not well regulated. The FDA makes claims that the food won't hurt us, but there exists little to no accountability for health claims if food manufacturers say the food helps us.

In our opinion, eating your vitamins and minerals the way Mother Nature packages them, in unprocessed whole foods, is optimum for health. If your specific physiology needs more nutrients of a certain type, compared to what you are able to get in your diet, then you should choose your own supplement, ensuring its quality and effectiveness. If you eat our recommended six-plus cups of vegetables a day you should be getting more than enough of most of your required nutrients.

If not dairy, then what?

As with gluten substitutes there are lots of healthy alternatives to consuming pasteurized cow dairy products. Depending on the laws in your state you may be able to find locally sourced raw milk. It is worth experimenting with this food to see if you can tolerate it as there are many health benefits (see www.realmilk.com for more information). Additionally, there are several other alternatives to cow dairy, some of which are used in the recipes of this book.

Dairy substitutes:
- Goat or sheep milk
- Rice milk
- Coconut milk
- Almond milk
- Hemp milk

We do not recommend soy products as an alternative to dairy. Soy products are some of the most heavily processed foods on the market today. Additionally, there is a lot of controversy around the issue of soy milk and whether it truly has health benefits or actually contributes to some disease states. Until the research on this topic becomes more clear we generally recommend avoiding the consumption of any soy products in your diet.

Food Guidelines

The following are the recommended eating guidelines that we offer to you to add health to your life. These tips are not to be confused with laws, rules, or dogma. If you can find a balance with food, your body will thank you with joy, freedom, energy, and health.

When we present these guidelines to our patients, some of them have the tendency to put the responsibility of their food choices back on us by saying, "My doctor won't let me eat _____," or, "I can't eat _____ because my doctor told me not to."

To them, and to any of you who have this tendency, we offer some very wise words from one of our greatest teachers, Dr. Liz Collins, ND: "If you can fit it in your mouth, you can eat it." You can eat anything. You can drink motor oil if you want, but you may not like the results. Remember, ultimately, what you put in your mouth is your choice, and the subsequent results are also your choice based on what you put in your mouth. We offer you these guidelines to add health to your life and to help you feel your best. Health is the result of making choices every day that are in alignment with what your body needs to thrive, and it can all start with food.

As you read this book, you may also notice we suggest using some of the ingredients we are telling you to avoid here. We tell you to avoid processed food, then include a list of resources to find gluten and dairy-free processed foods. That is because life is about balance, and fun! Some things, like goat cheese, white potatoes, and even carefully selected processed foods, have their place in our lives and on our plates, as long as they are used on occasion and not as a staple.

1. Eat whole foods.

Ideally eat organic, in-season, and locally grown whole foods. To find local food markets, grocery stores, and restaurants near you, visit www.localharvest.org.

Eating "whole" foods simply means that you are eating foods in their original form or close to it. When in doubt, ask yourself, "Would a caveman recognize this as food?" Besides your local farmers' market, you will find these foods around the periphery of the grocery store: the produce section, the meat counter, the fish counter, and the dairy section.

Examples of whole food versus processed food: whole oats versus Cheerios, brown rice versus white rice, vegetables versus V8, ground beef versus frozen burritos, fresh fish versus fish sticks, oranges versus orange juice.

Health tip: It takes at least eight oranges to make one glass of juice. Translation: for every glass of juice you drink, you consume at least eight times more sugar than you would by consuming the whole fruit. The detrimental effects of that amount of sugar in juice (even a "natural" sugar) far outweigh the claimed health benefits, not to mention, you lose the beneficial fiber as well.

There are many ways to eat fresh, local, organic produce affordably. Consider joining a CSA (community-supported agriculture group), shopping at farmers' markets, buying from the farmer directly, or planting a garden.

2. Eat vegetables

lots of vegetables. One-half to three-fourths of every meal should be vegetables. The more colorful each meal is, the better. In all your meals, include a variety of reds (for example, radishes, apples, peppers, beets), oranges (peppers, oranges, squash, yams), yellows (golden beets, beans, peppers, pineapple), greens, lots of greens (broccoli, peas, kale, chard, spinach, cabbage, brussels sprouts, beans), blues (blueberries, blackberries), and purples (eggplant, cabbage, onions, beans, cauliflower. Eat the colors of the rainbow; it's the best multivitamin there is!

3. Eat protein

at every meal. Adults should eat about twenty to thirty grams of protein at every meal. That is equivalent to three eggs or a three- to four-ounce portion of meat, about the size of a deck of cards. Choose fresh cold-water fish (halibut, salmon, sardines, anchovies, haddock, mackerel, trout), grass-fed beef, lamb, pork, wild game (elk, deer, turkey, pheasants, rabbit), chicken, or farm-raised eggs. Healthy protein supports balanced weight, mood, blood sugar, and hormones.

Find a farmer in your area that raises animals both humanely and on their natural diet. Buy directly from the farmer for cheaper prices and better quality. Visit: www.localharvest.org or www.eatwild.com.

4. Eat healthy fats.

Contrary to popular belief, too much fat does not make you fat (too much sugar does). Healthy fats are required for optimal health. Fats are essential for your brain, heart, and lung function, and to keep eyes and skin healthy. Many of our neurotransmitters and hormones are dependent on fat to be balanced and healthy. Thirty to 40 percent of your daily calories should be from fat (sixty to ninety grams for a two-thousand-calorie-a-day diet). One stick of butter contains eighty-eight grams of fat.

Healthy sources of fat include butter, olive oil, coconut milk and coconut oil, avocados, nuts and seeds, cold-water fish, and healthy meats as described above.

We exclusively use organic butter, cold-pressed olive oil, and coconut oil for cooking. Use olive or coconut oil for high-heat cooking.

5. Drink lots of water.

We recommend drinking half your body weight in ounces every day. Adequate intake of water is essential for proper elimination of toxins, mental function, and intercellular communication. The only beverages that count as water are water and unsweetened herbal tea. Coffee, caffeinated tea, sports drinks, alcohol, and fruit juice not only do not count as water, but they each also have their own detrimental effects on your health.

6. Add fresh herbs and spices to everything.

Include as many herbs and spices as possible in your dishes, because herbs and spices have many health benefits. Keep an eye out throughout this book for some of the many health-promoting benefits of herbs and spices in our recipes. Popular herbs include ginger, garlic, parsley, cilantro, basil, mint, sage, rosemary, thyme, turmeric, cumin, cinnamon, etc.

7. Use natural sweeteners in moderation.

Natural sweeteners include maple syrup, molasses, local honey, and fruit.

8. Eat whole, gluten-free (GF) grains in moderation.

Treat grains as a condiment to supplement your meat and veggies, not as a staple component of your caloric intake.

Suggested GF grains include wild rice, brown rice, buckwheat, steel-cut oats, quinoa, teff, millet, amaranth.

Delicious grain alternatives include starchy veggies, i.e., squash (of all types), turnips, parsnips, beets, rutabagas, yams, sweet potatoes, celery root, and pumpkin.

Avoid all gluten-containing grains, including wheat,

spelt, rye, barley, kamut, and all processed grains (grains that have been made into flours, i.e., all breads, pastas, and cereals).

9. *Avoid processed foods.*

While this is the flip side of "eat whole foods" and we are just saying it a different way, this is worth the statement and reiteration. We are raving fans of all kinds of foods…but these little buggers, "processed foods," aren't actually real food. Processed foods are actually food like substances masquerading as food and are mostly found in the middle aisles of the grocery story (hint: they come in a box, can, or plastic package, may be pasteurized or homogenized, and may have ingredients you can't pronounce). Eat whole foods; avoid processed food.

10. *Do not eat gluten, dairy, soy, high fructose corn syrup, and sugar.*

We have found these foods to be the most problematic for our patients in general, and their consumption displaces other more nutritious foods from our daily eating habits. If you are sitting down to a muffin for breakfast, it's a meal at which you didn't get enough protein, vitamins, and minerals. Whether or not you are actually allergic to these foods, they do cause inflammation in your body, and simply avoiding them adds health, and you will find yourself eating a lot of much healthier foods instead.

A Note about Sugar: It is true that cane sugar and high fructose corn syrup are essentially the same thing—they are both bad for you. Avoid cane sugar, white sugar, brown sugar, powdered sugar, turbinando sugar, corn syrup, high fructose corn syrup, fructose (unless in whole fruits), and agave. Yes, agave, too. It is a processed, unnatural food with a similar chemical profile as high fructose corn syrup.

Previously, we didn't include points nine and ten in our guidelines, as our philosophy is to focus on what adds health—healthy protein, fats, and lots of veggies—versus what creates disease. For some of us, though, ourselves included, it is helpful to cut to the chase and hear it, plain and simple. Whether you are allergic or sensitive to these foods or not, they are a major source of inflammation in everyone's body, and thus a major contributor to disease.

We are often asked how much of these foods is "OK" for your health. Well, we suppose the question is akin to: how many cigarettes are "OK" for your health? Although this one may seem harsh, we coach all our patients to listen to what their bodies are telling them. Symptoms and disease (pain, discomfort, disability, low energy, and emotional imbalance) are your body's way of trying to get your attention to change something you are currently doing that your body does not like. Learning to listen to your body is the key to a living a long and happy life. This takes getting quiet, slowing down, and the willingness to hear the truth.

PART III

"This is my invariable advice to people:
Learn how to cook-try new recipes, learn
from your mistakes, be fearless, and above
all have fun!" -Julia Child

RECIPES FOR SUCCESS

We want to set you up for success, so the next few sections are a really basic overview of the kitchen must-haves, stocking and shopping tips, and "the deal" with snacks. If you're new at this, or wherever you are in the process, take it one step at a time and have fun! A key component of adding health is that every aspect of food should be fun and enjoyable.

◆ KITCHEN BASICS ◆

Tools and Equipment

Having the right tools and equipment can mean the difference between a meal taking thirty minutes versus ninety. A food processor is worth the investment in how much you're going to save with all the homemade foods you can make with it.

Healthy storage options are another important tool for success. Glass Pyrex containers and mason jars make for quick and easy grabs in the morning for lunches or picnics. Always choose glass over plastic, always.

Cookware/Equipment

Stainless steel pots

One large stockpot

Stainless steel saucepan

Cast iron pans: griddles,
  skillets, and dutch ovens

Veggie steamer basket

Wood cutting boards
  *(wood is much healthier than plastic,
  being more antimicrobial)*

Food processor

Hand blender

Coffee grinder

Mason jars

Glass storage containers

Large serving platters

Large salad bowls

Citrus hand juicer, or "squisher,"
  as it is known in our kitchen

Egg poacher

Grater/zester

Sharp knives

Rubber spatula

Wooden spoons

Wire whisk

Knife sharpener

WHAT TO STOCK IN YOUR PANTRY

Sarah and I do pantry tours in our kitchen and pantry makeovers for our patients. What surprises most of our friends when they look in my pantry is the amount of room we have dedicated to plates, vases, pots, and pans, because the room isn't taken up by processed foods. We have two shelves stocked with canned tomatoes from last summer, vinegars, oils, canned beans, gluten-free snacks, and jars of rice, quinoa, nuts, and seeds.

Justin and I had a family friend stay with us for a few days recently. After she left, I got an e-mail saying that in the short time she spent in our house, watching us cook, opening our fridge, and looking in our pantry, her life was forever changed. When people see it being done and have the visceral experience, the shift in their own lives is made much easier. We will try to communicate this as much as possible through this book; however, if you live in Montana (or plan a visit), we invite you to our monthly dinners during the winter, or come visit us at the farmers' market in the summer. We would love to do whatever we can to facilitate this healthy transformation for you.

-Tanda

Here's a list of what we keep in our pantry, fridge, in the spice rack, and on the counter to add flavor, substance, and pizzazz to every meal:

In the Pantry

Raw, organic apple cider vinegar
White wine vinegar
Balsamic vinegar
Rice wine vinegar
Olive oil, cold-pressed organic
Worcestershire sauce
Honey
Butter *(it keeps well in the pantry in Montana, if in Florida you might want it in the fridge)*
Liquid Aminos
Tamari
Fish sauce
Red curry paste
Brown rice syrup
Coconut oil
Coconut milk
Gluten-free oats
Polenta
Quinoa
Brown rice
Wild rice
Gluten-free bread mix
Gluten-free pancake mix
Gluten free snacks—pretzels,
Pirate's Booty, corn chips, rice crackers
Seeds: sunflower, sesame, flax, pumpkin, poppy
Nuts: almonds, pine nuts, Brazil nuts, cashews, walnuts, pecans

In the spice rack

Sea salt
Pepper grinder with black peppercorns
Curry powder
Paprika
Cumin
Coriander
Ground white pepper
Dried thyme
Dried rosemary
Cinnamon
Nutmeg
Cayenne
Whole fennel seeds
Herbs de Provence
Cocoa powder
Turmeric
Italian seasoning mix
Cloves

In the fridge

Maple syrup
Sunflower butter
Almond butter
Extra butter
Hot chili sauce
Capers
Olives
Homemade hummus or bean dip
Farm-fresh eggs
Homemade mayonnaise
Homemade ketchup
Mustard

On the counter

Fresh cilantro, parsley, dill, mint in small vases
Bowl of fresh garlic
Large thumb of ginger
Bowl of onions, root veggies, winter squash, lemons, and limes
Bucket for kitchen scraps to feed the chickens
Compost bucket underneath the sink
Homemade salad dressings

GROCERY SHOPPING 101

Grocery shopping is one of my favorite pastimes and one I look forward to every week. When Justin and I lived in Portland, we would frequent the farmers' markets and local grocery stores, and my eyes would pore over the fresh produce and cuts of local meat; we'd fill our baskets and trot home with these slices of heaven. We often hear that grocery shopping is not a favorite pastime for people and that it can be intimidating, especially when you're trying to shift your focus to whole foods. Here are some tips and treasures to make it easier, more convenient, and, dare I say, fun.—Tanda

I remember the days of grocery shopping back when I was a vegetarian. It was easily a one-hour process, and often I went to several different stores until I found all the supplies I needed for the week. Since I changed the way I eat to whole foods, I can't remember a time I have spent more than 20 minutes in the store. And with a second freezer at home full of local meat, all I do is stop in the produce section, maybe dive down one aisle for a bottle of olive oil or can of coconut milk, and I am done. Ten minutes start to finish, even to feed a house full of guests.—Sarah

Shop the perimeter

The whole foods are typically located around the edges of the grocery store. The veggies, fruits, meat, eggs, and butter all lie around the perimeter, making it easy to cruise around the edges, fill your basket, and wind up at the checkout. The only reason to shop the middle is to stock or restock pantry items such as vinegars, oils, spices, and condiments.

Buy local, farm-raised when available

There are few things I enjoy more than wandering the weekly seasonal farmers' markets and watching the farmers, with their radiant faces, proudly handing over food that came from their hands and the land they've cultivated. In recent years it has become increasingly apparent to me how important it is to buy from these local farmers, not only for economy and conversation, but for your health, too.

Why buy local?
Here are just a few reasons:

Taste and Freshness

Local food tastes better (and is better for you). There's nothing like the taste of fresh fruits and veggies right off the vine, roots out of the ground, or fresh food straight out of the oven. Everybody knows that fresh food just tastes better. Shopping at local markets ensures that the tastes and textures you buy are sweet, flavorful, and true to nature.

Just Plain Healthier

When buying local, you can expect exceptional freshness and quality. Several studies have shown that the average distance a food travels from farm to plate is 1,500 miles; it can take a week or more for the food to reach your table (or fridge or pantry); and in that time, the sugars turn to starches, plant cells shrink, nutrients are lost, and the vitality of the produce is greatly diminished. Produce picked and consumed within a twenty-four-hour period is crisp, packed with vital nutrients, and loaded with flavor. Simply put, local food is just plain healthier. A shorter time and distance from farm to plate mean that those precious nutrients are still abundant and available to maximize your health.

Seasonal Eating and Connection with the Land

Buying locally grown food helps you eat with the rhythm of the seasons, and eating seasonally supports your health in numerous ways. Point of purchase, cooking fresh and eating local food creates a connection with your food and the land; it gives you an easy and natural method of eating with the seasons. You are able to gain a visceral appreciation of the weather, and personal insight into the miracles and challenges that come with growing and raising food.

Support and Stewardship

Buying locally grown foods supports your immediate community. By circulating your dollars within your community you personally strengthen your local economy, supporting growth and viability. You build a relationship between you, your community, and your farmers. Buying local foods supports the family farms in your region. Family farmers and ranchers are some of the best stewards of our land and resources; sustainable farms are a dying breed and need our support and stewardship. When a farmer is able to sell directly to the consumer, he or she is able to bypass the middleman, receiving the full retail price of his or her commodity. This means that farmers can afford to continue farming and doing the work that they love and loving the work that they do.

It's Easy

Buying locally is this easy: go to www.localharvest.com and www.eatwild.com and search for farmers and farmers' markets near you. We encourage you to go see, smell, and taste your local food, and to thank and shake the hand of your farmer.

Buying in Bulk and Owning a Freezer

A great way to eat royally year round and save cash at the same time is to buy in bulk in the summer months and preserve your bounty by freezing or canning for winter meals. Last summer, we split sixty pounds of tomatoes that we purchased from a local farmer. We spent one whole Sunday canning them so we could have fresh, summery tomatoes for soups, stews, sauces, and chili all winter long. Having a chest or stand-up freezer gives you the ability to preserve summer's food, stock meats, and have storage space for large batches of soups and stocks. Last fall Justin got an antelope, a deer, and an elk, and by midsummer we are more than halfway through it. We make our own breakfast sausage, burgers, jerky, and summer sausage. We pull them out year round for snacks, chili, grilling, and feeding groups as well as ourselves. If you or your partner hunts for wild game or if you find access to local meat in bulk, you will definitely need a freezer.

SNACKING TIPS

When we talk to people about eating whole food, questions around snacking inevitably arise, and it's really one of the first things people want to know about. Can I snack? Should I snack? When can I snack? What should I snack on? These are all great questions. Snacking is a great way to help balance blood sugar and prevent crashes, shakiness, and emotional roller-coasters. One of the keys to balancing blood sugar is snacking on protein.

The analogy we use is that eating protein is like throwing a log on a fire. It will burn steadily for a long time, akin to the kind of energy protein provides. Protein maintains stable blood sugar, and thus energy, for several hours. Conversely, reaching for highly processed carbohydrates and sugar to snack on is like throwing paper on a fire; it burns quickly and then it's gone. Our blood sugar spikes and then crashes, leading us to reach for more carbs and thus creating a damaging blood sugar cycle. And if you walk down the grocery aisle, most of the snack foods are highly processed and loaded with empty carbs, sugar, and sodium. But they don't have to be when you reach for whole foods to munch on.

Some people find they need to eat every two to three hours to prevent crashes, and if you're one of them, reach for snacks high in protein like jerky, meats, nuts, seeds, or wholesome leftovers. If you choose to have a high-carbohydrate or sugary snack, add some fat and protein to help stabilize the blood sugar effects and get the most out of your snack. Say you want an apple; instead of the plain apple, which is high in sugar, add some almond butter to it. If you want some crunchy rice crackers, dip them in hummus or bean dip (see page 192). Adding healthy protein also helps you crowd out less healthy snacks, helping to interrupt the snacking cycle so that you can sustain your blood sugar for longer lengths of time.

A great way to assure access to adequate, nourishing snacking material is to make it from scratch—a variety of proteins, protein bars, dips, and sauces can all be stored for quick and easy grabbing.

Other than meat, veggies, fruit, nuts, and seeds, many typical snack foods aren't so great for you. However, in moderation (i.e., a few times a week), many of these are perfectly healthy things to supplement your meals with.

All-you-can-eat snacks

• Leftovers

• Veggies—raw or lightly steamed (examples: avocados, broccoli, carrots, cauliflower, cabbage, zucchini, cucumbers, etc.)

• Homemade dips (examples: hummus, black bean dip, salsa, olive tapenade, tahini)

• Dip conduits: raw veggies, lightly steamed veggies

• Soups (ideally homemade)

• Bone broth (see page 148)

• Chopped up leftover meats, poultry, or fish

• Nuts and seeds

• Almond butter, sunflower seed butter, hazelnut butter, cashew, and macadamia nut butter (peanut butter is highly inflammatory and not recommended)

• Fruit (no more than one or two servings a day)

On-occasion snacks

• Dip conduits: corn chips, veggie chips, gluten-free crackers, gluten-free pretzels

• Jerky (ideally homemade from grass-fed beef or wild game)

• Deli meats and your favorite condiment—like stone-ground mustard!

• Trail mix with dried fruit

• Popcorn (make from scratch, not microwaveable, so you may choose the best oils and salt)

-Gluten-free cookies and other gluten-free sweet treats

• Dark chocolate and fresh fruit

• Dairy-free ice cream (see resources page 200)

SEASONAL SHOPPING

We talk a lot about whole foods, but what about eating with the seasons? We do a significant amount of education on the subject of eating with the seasons. Even if you only have access to the grocery store and don't have access to a farmers' market nearby, you can still shop with the seasons and eat seasonally appropriate foods. When you buy foods in season, they are fresher, contain more nutrients, and likely came from shorter distances because they can be grown closer to home.

Taking in seasonal food follows our bodies' natural rhythms and cravings. Craving cold beverages or fresh tomatoes and basil on a hot summer's day, and craving thick, warm soups and root vegetables on cold winter days, are examples of our body's wisdom and how our bodies crave foods with the season. Our bodies have different requirements at different times of the year, especially for natural cleansing and sustaining energy. Our seasonal cravings are evidence that our bodies know best and eating with the seasons is a great way to add health to your body all year round. Here's a really brief rundown of what to look for in spring, summer, fall, and winter.

Fall	Winter	Spring	Summer
Brussels sprouts	Winter squash	Asparagus	Tomatoes
Apples	Potatoes	Radishes	Corn
Pumpkins	Parsnips	Peas	Bell peppers
Squash	Turnips	Herbs	Raspberries
Cabbage	Rutabaga	Greens	Strawberries
Cauliflower	Sweet potatoes	Beets	Blueberries
Celeriac	Yams	Pea shoots	Cantaloupe
Sunchokes or Jerusalem artichokes	Kale	Artichokes	Cucumbers
	Mushrooms	Carrots	Eggplant
Parsnips	Pomegranates	Cherries	Garlic
Rutabaga	Leeks	Rhubarb	Onions
Turnips	Onions		Melons
			Zucchini
			Summer squash

EATING VEGETABLES

At Clearwater Healthcare we recommend every person eat five to six cups of vegetables a day. Here we share our favorite ways to prepare them and get them into our daily routines to make that happen:

Eat the colors of the rainbow

Select a wide variety of colors and types of fresh vegetables to ensure you are getting all the vitamins and minerals available to you. Every time you go to the store, try buying a vegetable you rarely or have never eaten before, and experiment to expand your knowledge and tastes. A great game to play, especially with kids, is to take the foreign food home and look it up on the Internet to see what it is and how it eat it. Eating the rainbow is the best multivitamin there is.

Storage know-how

To refrigerate or not to refrigerate? That is the question. The answer is, not all fruits and veggies need to be in the fridge. Many stay better tasting, and better for you, at room temperature. Onions, garlic, root vegetables, and squash can all stay out on the counter, in your pantry, or in the root cellar. Fruits and tomatoes also stay sweeter and more nutritious at room temperature. If you have a question about storage, look it up on the Internet; there is some wonderful information out there now to help answer the proverbial refrigeration question, and you may be surprised by some of the answers you find. Also, a great tip is to buy smaller quantities more often, to keep your portions fresh and nutritious.

Local over organic

Locally grown food is always the best choice, even over organic. A good time to buy organic foods is during the winter months when less local food is available.. If you cannot afford to buy all organic fruits and veggies, consult the annual report on the "Dirty Dozen" and the "Clean Fifteen" for lists of the most and least toxic conventionally grown produce. Go to www.ewg.org/foodnews/ for the most current lists. Generally, non-citrus fruits and leafy vegetables are the most heavily sprayed, as bugs, just like us, love their sweetness and delicate leaves.

Veggie exceptions

We are big fans of all veggies. However, we do recommend that you limit your consumption of white potatoes and corn (which is not actually a vegetable at all but a grain), as they have low nutrient values compared to their high levels of carbohydrates, and they spike blood sugar. Some people, especially those with chronic joint pain or inflammatory disorders, will want to limit their intake of fruits and vegetables in the nightshade family, as nightshades can trigger pain. The nightshade family includes tomatoes, white potatoes (not sweet potatoes), bell peppers, and eggplants.

Lastly, those with thyroid disorders should use caution with vegetables of the cruciferous family, as they can be harmful to the thyroid when eaten raw. The cruciferous vegetables include broccoli, cauliflower, brussels sprouts, white and purple cabbage, and bok choy. Please, do not stop eating these important veggies, just be sure to lightly cook them.

COOKING WITH KIDS

Getting your kids involved in the kitchen and meal prep can be one of the best ways to instill a healthy relationship with food for life. Food has a natural and amazing way of engaging and exciting all the senses. Cooking with children builds lifelong skills and provides an intimate space for dynamic hands-on learning.

Being included in healthy food preparation not only helps with healthy brain development, but focuses energy and attention, balances mood, helps build social skills, allows creativity to bloom, builds self-esteem and self-reliance, and instills a sense of personal responsibility, knowledge, and respect for what they themselves are putting into their bodies.

Here are some ideas for getting kids in the kitchen, engaged, and excited about healthy food and being healthy.

Safety First

Educate your kids about safety in the kitchen. Let them know about hot stoves, sharp knives, and boiling water. No horsing around, and wash those hands.

Keep Them Involved

Kids love helping. They appreciate a job and like to feel important. Have them wash veggies, rip lettuce, mix and measure things. Find age-appropriate tasks so they love cooking with you and don't get frustrated. Have them read the recipe to you or help you get out pots, pans, lids, and utensils; this will also help them learn their way around the kitchen.

Ask your kids questions while you're working, like "what's your favorite meal?" Ask about shapes, colors, names, and textures.

Taste Testing

This is the best part! Ask their opinion, if the dish needs anything, or if it's too hot or too cold. You can also make a game out of this; you can cut up a group of different fruits and veggies, have them taste each one, and then pick their favorite.

Eat the Colors of Rainbow

Eat all the colors of the rainbow because it's the best multivitamin there is! Look for red beets; red cabbage; orange squash and orange root vegetables; red, orange, and yellow peppers; yellow, orange, and purple carrots; yellow and purple cauliflower; purple potatoes; and green everything! You can even cook onions and root vegetables like turnips, parsnips, and yams with beets, and the red beet juice will turn the other veggies red, too!

Give Them Choices

Kids love to have choices. Ask them before you get started if they'd like broccoli or carrots, beef or venison, one or two. Give them the choices you would like them to have.

Spice It Up!

Don't be afraid to add a little spice to any meal. Try cilantro, parsley, mint, or basil in the summer, or herb it up with rosemary, thyme, and sage in the winter. Try some turmeric on your veggies, rice, or eggs; it will turn things bright yellow, which could be really fun. (Caution: a little turmeric goes a long way, and it also stains.) Little fingers also love to pick fresh herbs from kitchen pots and herb gardens, so start a kitchen herb garden and have your children help you harvest a little bit before every meal.

Lead by Example

Kids pay attention to what you do and how you do it. So if you "hate" veggies or groan about eating broccoli, most likely your kids will, too. Prepare meals that you love so that they learn happy, healthy eating habits. They will learn to love good food by watching you enjoy it, too.

Take Them to the Grocery Store

Help them make a list and, depending on their age, give them a basket, too; some grocery stores even have mini shopping carts for the little "shoppers in training." Teach them where the whole foods live, on the periphery of the store, and encourage them to choose foods in their natural form. A few moments of each shopping trip dedicated to helping little ones learning about healthy foods are invaluable.

Beyond the Grocery Store

Take your kids to a local farm or farmers' market so they can see where food comes from, and introduce them to what goes into growing and harvesting what we eat. Many farms welcome children and families and have days dedicated to "picking your own" to encourage families to get their hands dirty. Kids are far more likely to eat fruits and veggies that they personally got to pull from the plant or pluck from the tree.

Make it Fun

Use different tools, shapes, textures, patterns, arrangements, and combinations. Get the cookie cutters out and, instead of shaping dough, use them on eggplants, potatoes, yams, sweet potatoes, winter squash, and zucchinis. There are endless playful veggie ideas out there to experiment with, and making veggies fun is a great way to get them into your kids' mouths!

Five Meal Ideas for Kiddos

1. Make-your-own-burrito bar. Prepare a spread of beans, salsa, ground meat, shredded lettuce, and guacamole. Use gluten-free wraps or corn tortillas and let them make their own.

2. Make-your-own-gluten-free pizza. Everyone chooses their toppings and personalizes their pizza with patterns. See references for great gluten-free product options (reference section page 200).

3. Use spaghetti squash in place of pasta. The texture is very similar, and it's much higher in vitamins and minerals, not to mention spaghetti squash is a whole food, hasn't been processed, and it's really fun, even for us big kids. Make a traditional spaghetti sauce and ladle it over this delicious vegetable (see Spaghetti Squash with Italian Sausage recipe, page 91)

4. Creamy soups. Bet you are wondering how we cream soups without dairy? We use coconut milk, almond milk, butter, and pureed white or sweet potatoes. Experiment with different colors of creamy soups, like creamy purple soup using purple cauliflower that's steamed or boiled and pureed with butter and cream. Use carrots, beets, or peas for orange, red, or green creamy soups. Creamy, colorful soups are great way to get veggies in, especially if kids have a hard time with the textures of certain steamed, fresh raw, or roasted veggies. (see the Creamy Tomato Bisque recipe for more ideas, page 153)

5. Add a little bacon or goat cheese. Let's face it, everything tastes better with bacon and cheese. Toss some pancetta or crumbled bacon pieces into sautéed kale, or melt goat cheese over steamed cauliflower or zucchini.

PART IV

"All I ever wanted to do was to make food accessible to everyone; to show that you can make mistakes-I do all the time but it doesn't matter."-Jamie Oliver

THE RECIPES

BREAKFAST

The age-old wisdom that breakfast is the most important meal remains as true today as ever, which is why breakfast gets its very own section of this book. Eating a healthy breakfast is essential to live a healthy lifestyle. The opposite of eating a healthy breakfast, skipping breakfast, is one of the worst things you can do for your health. Skipping breakfast or eating a high-carb, high-sugar breakfast increases our waistlines, decreases our energy level, and leads to poor sleep patterns, hormone imbalances, and even mood disorders like anxiety and depression. Eating a healthy breakfast can increase your metabolism encouraging your body to actually burn more fat, stabilize blood sugar reducing midafternoon energy crashes and trips to the refrigerator or coffee shop, and decrease portion sizes at lunch and dinner because you won't feel as hungry. Unfortunately, the all-American breakfast has also led us astray. When most Americans think of breakfast, they think cereal and milk, bagels and cream cheese, pancakes, French toast, waffles, pastries, or, as is often the case, a triple venti vanilla low-fat latte. When really pressed to think of a healthy breakfast, there is usually fruit and oatmeal involved, and often extra sugar. However, at their molecular core, all of these foods are mostly sugar. Grains break down into glucose (a sugar), fruit into fructose (a sugar), milk into lactose (a sugar), not to mention the added sugar in processed foods. This is a setup for weight gain, low, sluggish metabolism, and an energy crash midafternoon. Add a cup of blood-sugar-spiking coffee and you have a recipe for a health disaster.

When we recommend that our patients eliminate gluten and dairy from their diet, the typical first question we get is, "But what do I eat for breakfast?" In our houses we pretty much always eat some variation of The Usual (see page 54) at least five days a week, adding in the occasional protein smoothie, and save more complex breakfasts like Huevos Rancheros (see page 62) or GF pancakes (see page 63) for lazy weekend mornings. However, breakfast always consists of some sort of protein with additional veggies and healthy fats.

When we do want a more traditional American breakfast, there are lots of wonderful gluten-free, grain-based products out there to choose from—everything from gluten-free pancake and muffin mixes to premade bagels and breads. All are a great treat on occasion, especially when served with a helping of pasture- raised butter. See our product resources information in the appendix.

RECIPES

OPEN-FACE EGG AND SAUSAGE STACK

INGREDIENTS

2 organic sausage patties

2 slices of your favorite
gluten-free toast

1 avocado

2 thick slices of fresh tomato

1 tablespoon organic butter

2 farm-fresh eggs

Sea salt and freshly ground
pepper to taste

Fresh basil, cilantro, or dill
for garnish

Serves 1 - 2

In a nonstick frying pan over medium, heat cook the sausage patties, then set aside on your breakfast plate. Toast the two pieces of bread. Scoop and spread half of the avocado on each piece. Place a slice of tomato on top of the avocado, and a sausage patty on top of that. Reduce the heat in the pan to medium-low, add the butter, and when the butter stops foaming, crack the eggs into the pan; cook about 2 minutes, then flip and cook another minute for "over easy." Remove the eggs from the pan and place them on top of the sausage patties, then season with salt and pepper and sprinkle with an herb garnish.

Try This:
Make you own GF bread in a bread maker or bake in the oven; slice and freeze for later use. (See resources section for GF bread mixes page 200).

Health Tip:
Locally raised farm eggs from chickens that are truly free range have a higher omega-3 to omega-6 ratio associated with decreased inflammation, less cholesterol, and more brain-healing beta-carotene than the conventionally raised store-bought alternatives.

One Saturday morning I was in the beginning stages of making breakfast, and I asked Justin how he wanted his eggs. "Fried, please," he said, so this is what I came up with, and now it is a frequent morning request of his.

-Tanda

THE USUAL

INGREDIENTS

¼ cup organic breakfast sausage

1 tablespoon organic butter

1 clove garlic, chopped

1 cup assorted veggies, chopped (see variations)

2 farm-fresh eggs

Fresh cilantro to garnish

Sea salt and freshly ground pepper to taste

Serves 1

Variation 1:

Red onion, bell pepper, broccoli, fresh snap peas, sliced carrot

Variation 2:

Leftover roasted beets, sweet potatoes, and parsnips, with red cabbage and brussels sprouts

Variation 3:

Leftover squash, carrots, parsnips, spinach, and celery

Variation 4:

Red onion, broccoli, cauliflower, mushrooms, and chard

Varaiation 5:

Red onion, mushrooms, extra garlic, halved cherry tomatoes, and spinach

In a frying pan over medium heat, cook the breakfast sausage (you can cook it as a patty or break it up into smaller pieces). When it's fully cooked, melt the butter in the pan and add the veggies. Cook until tender (5–7 minutes), and place in a breakfast bowl. Add any precooked veggies or greens in the last 2–3 minutes.

It's easiest to poach the eggs with an egg poacher if you have one (you can also use custard cups or something equivalent). If not, poaching in a pan is easy. Fill a saucepan about halfway with water, add 1 tablespoon of white vinegar, and when the water begins to boil, crack the eggs into the water and bring the temp down to medium heat. Cook for 4½ minutes. Remove with a slotted spoon and place on a paper towel to dry. Add eggs to your breakfast bowl of veggies, season with salt and pepper, garnish with cilantro and enjoy!

Try This:

Try adding spices such as cumin, turmeric, or chili powder. You can also add ground seeds or hot sauce. This is also one of our favorite ways to use up leftover veggies from dinner. Anything roasted is delicious in this one.

Health Tip:

Eggs are one of our favorite foods. They have high-quality protein and contain essential fatty acids. They also contain choline, which helps reduce inflammation and helps keep the brain and nervous system healthy.

Weekends are the time for my husband and me to play with variations of "The Usual." Here are a few ways to get creative with "The Usual" breakfast of eggs, sausage, and veggies. Play around with this one; you may surprise yourself.

-Tanda

TWO-EGG OMELET WITH THICK-CUT BACON AND VEGGIES

INGREDIENTS

2 farm-fresh eggs

Sea salt and freshly ground pepper to taste

2 slices thick-cut bacon, chopped into bite-size pieces

¼ cup onion, chopped

¼ cup tomato, chopped

¼ cup spinach

2 mushrooms, chopped

1 tablespoon organic butter

¼ cup fresh herb of choice: basil, cilantro, dill, or parsley

Serves 1

In a small bowl, beat together the 2 eggs and season lightly with salt and pepper; set aside.

In a nonstick skillet with a tight-fitting lid, cook the bacon over medium heat, then add all of the veggies and sauté for 3–4 minutes, or until soft. Transfer bacon and veggies to a mixing bowl and set aside. Reduce heat to medium-low. Add the butter to the pan, and when it stops foaming, add the eggs; make sure the eggs cover the whole inside of the skillet. Add the veggie/bacon mixture to one half of the pan, cover with the lid, and let cook for 3–5 minutes or until the egg is mostly cooked and fluffed up. With a spatula fold the omelet in half and cook for another minute. Transfer to a plate, sprinkle herb of choice on top, and add freshly ground pepper.

Try This:

Breakfast for dinner, or lunch. These omelets make a great, quick, and savory dinner. Or make a 3-egg omelet and eat half for breakfast and save half for the next day or an easy to-go lunch.

Health Tip:

When shopping for bacon, it is worth choosing organic. All mammals, pigs included, tend to concentrate toxins in their fat. It is worth the extra couple of dollars to ensure your bacon is as toxin free as possible.

Here it is again, another version of our usual: veggies, eggs, and breakfast meats. This is a great Monday morning special to get your week started right. It's fun to play around with different combinations of veggies, styles of eggs, and fresh herbs for different taste delights.

-Sarah

SCRAMBLED EGG AND VEGGIE WRAP

INGREDIENTS

3 farm-fresh eggs

1 tablespoon organic butter

1 cup of veggies of your choice, chopped *examples*: onions, cabbage, spinach, mushrooms, tomatoes, parsnips, carrots, broccoli, cauliflower, asparagus, brussels sprouts, summer squash, or celery

1 brown rice or corn tortilla

1 handful of fresh cilantro, roughly chopped

Sea salt and freshly ground pepper to taste

Serves 1

In a small bowl beat the eggs and set aside.

In a nonstick skillet over medium heat, add the butter; when it's melted, add the chopped vegetables and sauté for 3–5 minutes or until tender. Add the eggs; reduce the heat to medium-low. With a spatula, stir and flip the eggs frequently until they have cooked evenly, about 4 minutes. When the eggs are done, place the eggs and veggie scramble on the rice or corn tortilla and garnish with chopped cilantro. Salt and pepper to taste.

Try This:

If you can tolerate it, this recipe is great with a few tablespoons of goat chevre (cheese) spread on the tortilla before adding the hot eggs and veggies. We love the chevre we get from our local goat dairy, Amalthia Farms, of the Gallatin Valley.

Health Tip:

All mammals store extra toxins in their fat. Therefore, it is a best health practice to choose organic fats, such as organic butter and olive oil, to ensure their quality.

During the summer my husband works two hours from home in the town of West Yellowstone. On Monday mornings he wakes at the crack of dawn to drive to his office there, so anything we can do to make his mornings go faster, the better. I make this breakfast for him on Sunday night and wrap it in tinfoil, throw it in the fridge, and it's a grab and go for him in the morning. It's also great fresh.

-Tanda

INSIDE-OUT OMELET

INGREDIENTS

3 farm-fresh eggs

½ cup rice milk

2 tablespoons organic butter or olive oil

2 cups kale, thinly chopped

1 cup broccoli, chopped into small florets

4–5 mushrooms; crimini or baby portabellas are delicious

½ red pepper, diced

¼ cup onion, finely chopped

2 cloves garlic, minced

3 tablespoons homemade pesto (see page 142 & 143)

Serves 2, or makes 2 days of breakfasts

Crack eggs into a small mixing bowl and beat with rice milk to a pale yellow. Heat a cast iron (or nonstick) griddle to medium heat, and a medium-large sauté pan to medium-high heat at the same time. Add 1 tablespoon oil or butter to each and warm or melt. Add all the veggies and the garlic to the sauté pan. Sauté until broccoli is softened but still crisp (about 3 minutes).

While the veggies are cooking, pour the eggs onto the griddle and cover with a lid (the lid prevents you from needing to flip the omelet). The eggs should be just done at the same time as the veggies, but be sure to check the eggs halfway through.

Turn off heat to both pans. Add pesto to middle of cooked eggs and fold each side into the center, overlapping them into thirds. Place on plate and top with veggies.

Try This:

Make this breakfast for two, or save half for tomorrow.

Health Tip:

Farm-raised, free-range eggs are an incredible source of beta-carotene, an antioxidant that prevents cancer, repairs damaged cells, and helps our body detoxify. They are also high in the antioxidant, fat-soluble vitamins A, D, and E, which are also anti-inflammatory, anti-cancer, great for brain function and mood stability, and can help heal heart disease.

I was sitting at the office one morning when Sarah came in with a delicious grin on her face. "What did you create?" I asked. She sat down in the chair across from me and told me about this inside-out concoction. She had me convinced, so I went home and tried it the next morning. The pesto takes an omelet and turns it up a few notches. When it is plated, it looks like a pile of eggy-veggie sautéed deliciousness. And trust us, it is.

-Tanda

GLUTEN-FREE OATMEAL BREAKFAST

INGREDIENTS

3 cups water

1 cup GF steel-cut oats

1 cup So Delicious Coconut Milk or ½ cup canned coconut milk

½ teaspoon cinnamon

½ teaspoon sea salt

2 tablespoon organic butter

Optional toppings

2 cups fresh berries

½ cup raisins

1 sliced apple or pear

Serves 4

Bring water to a boil, then add oats, coconut milk, cinnamon, and salt. Reduce heat and cook at a simmer for 25–30 minutes, until creamy. Stir in butter at end of cooking.

Serve with all-natural breakfast sausage, or with bacon (4–5 links of sausage or 8–10 pieces of bacon to serve 4).

Try This:
Steel-cut oats can take up to 30 minutes to cook. To save some time, cook oats in a larger batch and save in the fridge to reheat in the morning. Do not precook the sausage or bacon, as the fats can turn rancid in the fridge overnight.

Health Tip:
The addition of fat, coconut milk, and butter to these carbohydrates will lengthen the time it takes for the sugars to be released into your blood stream and thus limit a spike in blood sugar and the subsequent crash. The addition of fatty protein does the same, giving you a long-term energy source from a meal that normally burns off quickly.

We often get the question about whether or not oatmeal is gluten-free. The answer is yes, pure oats are gluten-free, but the caveat is that there can be cross-contamination from shared processing equipment. You have to buy oats that specifically say "gluten-free" on the package, because most oats and oat products are processed in factories which also process gluten-containing grains. So, read your labels.
-Sarah

GREEN EGGS AND HAM

INGREDIENTS

6 farm-fresh eggs

½ pound of country sausage or country ham

1 tablespoon organic butter

4 cloves garlic, chopped

2 cups fresh greens, chopped (spinach, kale, chard, beet greens, kohlrabi, turnip greens, bok choy, collards, or watercress)

¼ cup fresh cilantro, roughly chopped

Sea salt and freshly ground pepper to taste

Serves 3, or makes 3 days of breakfasts

Crack eggs into a small bowl and whisk; set aside. In a frying pan over medium-high heat, cook the sausage or brown the ham, and when it's cooked put it in a bowl and set aside. Turn down the heat to medium and add the butter and chopped garlic and sauté for 1 minute. Add the greens and sauté for another 2–4 minutes or until the greens are wilted. Add the eggs, ham or sausage, cilantro, salt, and pepper. Continue to stir and flip eggs until they are cooked through, about 5 minutes. Serve hot.

Try This:

Try adding goat cheese, other herbs such as parsley or basil, or spices such as cumin, paprika, or curry powder. Try it with chopped-up bacon bits or elk sausage.

Health Tip:

Tryptophan is the highest concentrated amino acid in eggs and is the precursor to serotonin, an important neurotransmitter that gives us our sense of well-being, confidence, and ease with life.

Every winter, a group of us would take a break from medical school and go play in Bend, Oregon, where we would rent a house and spend the weekend laughing, playing games, skiing, sledding, and, of course cooking. This was a breakfast one morning that all of us were "oohing" and "ahhing" over. I had brought some fresh bacon from a local farmer that was the perfect balance of smoky and salty, which gave this dish and extra kick. We like this one not just because of its title, but because of all the greens it gets us to eat.

-Tanda

SMOKED SALMON ON RICE CAKES

INGREDIENTS

1 ounce chevre goat cheese, a soft, cream-cheese-like goat cheese

2 rice or corn cakes

4 ounces smoked salmon

Optional toppings

Chives, chopped

Baby salad mix or baby spinach

Hard-boiled eggs, chopped

Pickles, sweet or dill, chopped

Capers

Fruit preserves -grape or dark fruits go well with baby spinach

Lemon wedge

Serves 1

Spread chevre cheese on rice or corn cake, add salmon, and top with favorite toppings.

Try This:

This breakfast can also make a great appetizer, lunch, or midday snack.

Health Tip:

Smoked fish may be rare on the American breakfast table, but it is a standard excellent source of morning protein, omega-3 essential fatty acids, and fat-soluble vitamins like A, D, and E, which all support immunity, brain health, and heart health.

When you're not in the mood for eggs, this is a great way to get a good source of protein and omega-3s to start your morning. Adding dill and capers or sweet pickles are key here.

-Tanda

HUEVOS RANCHEROS

INGREDIENTS

2 tablespoon apple cider vinegar

1 tablespoon organic olive oil

1 medium yellow onion, diced

4 cloves garlic, minced

1 (14 ounce) can stewed tomatoes

1 (14 ounce) can black beans

1 teaspoon ground cumin

1 teaspoon sea salt

6–12 farm-fresh eggs, depending on whether your crowd wants 1 or 2 eggs apiece

6 corn tortillas

6 large sprigs cilantro, for garnish

Serves 3–6

Put a medium saucepan of water on high heat, add vinegar, and bring to a boil. While the water is heating up, heat a second medium-sized saucepan to medium heat for the sauce. Add olive oil and warm it slightly, then add onion and garlic and sauté until onion is translucent (about 5 minutes). Then add the cans of tomatoes and beans, including the liquids. Season with cumin and salt and bring to a slow simmer while you poach the eggs. Stir occasionally.

At this point your water should be boiling for the eggs (see The Usual recipe for directions on poaching, page 54).

Lightly toast the tortillas in dry fry pan for 1 minute per side. Place each hot tortilla on a plate, and top with the tomatoes and bean sauce, a poached egg or two, and sprig of fresh cilantro. Serve.

Try This:

This sauce can be made ahead of time for a faster morning. Or, if you have leftovers, it makes a great dip with corn chips. Alternatively, if you have leftover chili (see page 154), you can use that in place of the sauce for a different version of this recipe.

Health Tip:

In general, Mexican food is already gluten-free and can be easily adapted to be dairy-free. This breakfast is often offered on the menus of more traditional American breakfast eateries and is a great alternative to wheat pancakes and eggs.

Every summer, beginning when I was six years old, my family would pack up the van and drive to the Adirondacks in upstate New York, where my parents' best friends had a camp. As we all got older, more and more traditions were created around food and special meals we prepared. This is one of the signature breakfasts whose scents would waft through our cabin windows, along with the sounds of Dad clanging in the kitchen, in the early hours of summer mornings. A fun hint with this one is to make our Summer Tomato Salsa (see page 178) the night before, for an appetizer, and make extra to use in this dish.

-Tanda

GLUTEN-FREE PANCAKE BREAKFAST

INGREDIENTS

1 cup Pamela's GF pancake mix (see resources for more info page 200)

5 farm-fresh eggs

1¼ cups rice milk

1 tablespoon organic butter, melted

½ pound all-natural nitrate-free bacon

Vermont maple syrup

Serves 2

Preheat oven to 400°F.

Whisk pancake mix, 1 egg, rice milk, and melted butter in a medium bowl until smooth, but do not overwhisk. Heat your favorite pancake pan (mine is a 31-year-old, 12-inch, cast iron griddle my mom gave me when I moved out for college) over medium heat.

While your beloved pancake pan is heating, arrange the bacon on a baking sheet, one strip next to another. Place the baking sheet onto the center rack of oven (even if it is not done preheating). Cook bacon just under desired crispiness (about 15–20 minutes).

While the bacon is cooking in the oven, cook pancakes until golden brown on both sides. Check bacon. If done, turn off oven and place cooked pancakes on another baking sheet and put them in the oven to keep warm while you cook the remaining 4 eggs to order (fried, scrambled, or poached).

Try This:

Make extra cakes and top with your favorite nut butter for a midday snack or after-dinner treat. Also, feel free to experiment with fruit such as blueberries, bananas, or homemade applesauce cooked into the cakes. A fun trick that my dad would do is put a little 1-inch slice of bacon in the middle of each pancake (or waffle) for a surprise center. The sweet and salty contrast is "to die for."

Health Tip:

Enjoy life! It is the opinion of these doctors that life is too short to never enjoy your favorite things. Going gluten free was a big transition for me, and one of the things I missed the most was my Sunday morning pancakes. The discovery of Pamela's GF pancake mix (see resources page 200) changed my whole world. What are your favorite usually non-gluten containing treats? Look for a tasty alternative out there, and don't forget to enjoy this life you are living!

It's a traditional pancake breakfast every Sunday morning at Justin's parents' house in upstate New York, and when I went gluten-free, so did his mom. So we shopped around for the best gluten-free pancake mix, and Pamela's won by a long shot. Be sure and drizzle lots of real maple syrup on top. I'm partial to Vermont's maple syrup because it's what my taste buds grew up on.

-Tanda

SMOOTHIES

A Note About Protein Powders:

Many conventional powders on the market today are whey (dairy) or soy based. We recommend avoiding both of these foods as they are common allergens and can be sources of chronic inflammation. Instead look for soy-free and dairy-free products such as rice, hemp, pea, egg white, or goat milk protein powders.

THE ULTIMATE SMOOTHIE

INGREDIENTS

1 cup So Delicious Coconut Milk
or ½ cup canned coconut milk

1 cup ice

1 cup baby spinach

1 cup frozen berries (blueberries, raspberries, blackberries, etc.)

1 serving protein powder (about 20 grams)

2 tablespoons ground flax, chia, or sunflower seeds (grind in a coffee grinder just before using to preserve quality of essential fatty acids)

1 serving your favorite powdered probiotic supplement

Combine all ingredients in a blender and blend until smooth and creamy. Add water if you desire thinner consistency.

Try This:
Try other berries or fruits, such as mango, papaya, kiwi, or melon.

Health Tip:
Although protein shake mixes are not a whole food, compared to other foods one might grab on the go, they make a great healthy alternative. The real goal is to not even need to have these around, but for most of us who might be prone to skip a meal, or to snack on cheese and crackers while making dinner (like me), mixing up a quick shake will do your body good.

Smoothies are one of our favorite quick and easy ways to get optimal nutrition in the morning. Smoothies can include protein, healthy fats, veggies, greens, and antioxidants. You can load your smoothies up with greens that you wouldn't otherwise eat during the day. They also make a great lunch substitute if you're on the go or know you're going to be somewhere where there aren't a lot of healthy options. One of our friends makes two smoothies at night: one she puts in the fridge for the morning and the other she puts in the freezer for her lunch to guarantee no blood sugar crashes throughout the day.
-*Tanda*

A GREEN SMOOTHIE

INGREDIENTS

1 pear

Juice of 1 lemon

2 large handfuls of baby spinach

1 cup pineapple juice

1 cup So Delicious Coconut Milk
or ½ cup canned coconut milk

1 serving protein powder (about 20 grams)

Combine ingredients in a blender and blend until smooth and creamy.

Try This:
If you are a bit adventurous in the kitchen, try adding ¼ cup packed cilantro or flat-leaf parsley to this smoothie. I dare you to try it—you will hardly taste it and it adds tons of essential nutrients (see health tip below).

Health Tip:
Green leafy vegetables are the most power-packed, nutrient-dense foods we eat. They are full of detoxifying chlorophyll; essential minerals such as iron, calcium, potassium, and magnesium; and vitamins, including K, C, E, and many of the B vitamins.

The lemon juice in this one keeps the greens from oxidizing. They look electric they are so bright. I brought this smoothie into the office one day and a patient looked at it and exclaimed, "What is that?" Then I had her taste it. Shocked and delighted, she started making them every day at home.
-*Sarah*

FRESH BANANA STRAWBERRY SMOOTHIE

INGREDIENTS

1 banana

4–5 large strawberries

1 cup So Delicious Coconut Milk or ½ cup canned coconut milk 1 cup ice

1 serving protein powder (about 20 grams)

Combine ingredients in a blender and blend until smooth and creamy.

Try This:

Make 2 servings first thing in the morning and place one in the freezer while you finish getting ready. Take the partially frozen smoothie on the go with you for a quick lunch or post workout recharge. In the summer, buy extra strawberries from local farmers and freeze for later use.

Health Tip:

Coconut milk has beneficial fiber for gastrointestinal health; it also boasts anti-cancer properties, antimicrobial properties, and protects us from diabetes. Coconut milk's medium-length fats provide instant energy, as they are absorbed directly into the bloodstream, unlike the longer fats from other plant oils such as canola, sunflower, and soy.

A quick and easy taste delight. I freeze bananas whole in their peels. When I want to use one in a smoothie, I put it in a glass of warm water for about 30 seconds. The peel comes right off and the frozen banana gives smoothies a great creamy texture.
-Sarah

CHOCOLATE ALMOND BUTTER SMOOTHIE

INGREDIENTS

1 serving (20 grams) chocolate protein powder, or 1 serving vanilla and 2 tablespoons cocoa powder

1 frozen banana

2 tablespoons almond or sunflower butter

1 cup rice milk

1 cup ice

Really kick up the health potential with:

2 tablespoons ground flax seeds (grind in coffee grinder)

1 serving your favorite powdered probiotic supplement

2 drops liquid vitamin D

Blend all ingredients in blender until smooth. Add additional water to desired consistency if necessary.

Try this:

One of my favorite kitchen tools is an electric hand blender. I make my smoothies in a 1-quart jar by adding all the ingredients and blending right in the jar for a no-mess, superfast meal. Toss on a metal lid and it won't spill in your bag or car on the way to work.

Health tip:

Why don't we use peanut butter?

Peanut butter can often be a hidden allergen for many people, and even if it is not, it is a source of inflammation that can exacerbate joint pain, arthritis, and other inflammatory conditions. Best health choices are almond, sunflower seed, cashew, macadamia nut, or hazelnut butters.

OK, this smoothie is so decadent it should be in the dessert section, but we don't have one, so here you go. One night after dinner my taste buds were in a fight with my brain to go find Ben and Jerry's Peanut Butter Cup Ice Cream. My healthy brain won out and this was the delicious result.
-Sarah

THE MAIN COURSE

In general, we follow a standard formula to design our lunches and dinners that is consistent with the Whole Food Plate (see page 19). In its essence, two-thirds of our plate is made up of two vegetable dishes (see the sections on vegetable sides, soups, salads, and appetizers and snacks for ideas). The other third comes from this section, "The Main Course," and is primarily some form of meat, poultry, or fish.

The main course is typically what the rest of the meal is built around in terms of complementary flavors, textures, and color. Food should taste good, and it should also look good. Taking time to plate food with love and artistry can actually add significant health to your meal. Preparing, touching, smelling and thinking about food all send signals to your brain that food is coming and your stomach actually begins to secrete digestive juices ahead of time. Just by looking at a beautiful meal your body will be more prepared to absorb all the nutrients available from the food in it.

Additionally, taking the time to slow down, relax, chew your food, and enjoy your meal with family and friends adds health to your life not only in terms of happiness and enjoyment, but also because eating in a relaxed environment allows your body to fully digest the food.

Dinner is our favorite meal for exactly that reason; it brings people together. Friends and family gather over a table with platters of meat, bowls of fresh veggies and greens, and bottles of local wine. Conversation flows, stories are told, and laughter rings throughout the house. As for lunch, following a gluten- and dairy-free lifestyle tends to pose a few challenges for our patients. Out goes the grab-and go sandwich and in comes leftovers from last night's dinner. When thinking about lunch, look to the soups, salads, and appetizers and snacks sections for even more ideas beyond leftover dinner. The key to lunch is planning. If it's not planned, we find ourselves reaching for fast food, processed food, or no food at all, none of which are good options. This really is the easiest meal of the day, as long are you make a little extra dinner or spend a Sunday afternoon roasting chicken or making a big pot of soup or chili.

Even though it may just be me, whenever I cook chicken I always cook a whole one, whether I roast it or cut it up and throw it on the grill. I use the leftovers to make chicken salad (see page 76), shredded in ginger sesame slaw (see page 167), or to make gluten-free chicken soup (see page 149).—Sarah

Growing up, dinner was the time when our whole family came together to talk about school and friends and got told repeatedly to chew with our mouths closed. In a conversation I had with my dad only a few years ago, he told me that every morning on his bike ride he would design dinner, the meal to nourish his family. It gave me a glimpse into what food meant to him, how much he loved it, and how it was his art.

Now I find myself doing the exact same thing every morning. On my drive into work, I design dinner. I can see the finished plate of perfectly grilled chicken, a summer salad with nasturtiums from the planters on our front porch, and roasted spring asparagus with coarse sea salt and freshly ground black pepper (see page 109). When I get home Justin starts the grill and I chop away. He sets the table on our front porch, where we can watch the sun set over our four horses grazing in the pasture. We catch up on the day, talk about life, our goals, and give thanks for where we are and what we have created. Some of my most memorable conversations have happened around the dinner table and candlelight.

-Tanda

RECIPES

SUMMER SAGE GRILLED PORK CHOPS
WITH GOAT CHEESE AND CARAMELIZED ONIONS

INGREDIENTS

4 organic pork chops

1 large handful of fresh
sage, finely chopped

Sea salt

Fresh ground white pepper

1 recipe of caramelized
onions (see page 121)

Goat chevre
(or goat cheese of choice)
to sprinkle on top

Serves 4

Rub both sides of the pork chops with fresh sage and then season with sea salt and white pepper. Let chops sit at room temp for 5–10 minutes.

Start the onions when you light the grill. Follow the recipe for caramelized onions (see page 121).

For the pork chops: Preheat the grill, place the seasoned chops on the grill, and cook for about 5 minutes on each side for medium doneness.

Arrange the pork chops on a plate, top with the caramelized onions, and sprinkle with the goat chevre.

Combine these with a fresh garden salad, steamed greens, grilled veggies, wild rice, roasted summer squash, or boiled salt potatoes for a fabulous easy meal for one or a whole group.

Try This:
Add fresh herbs such as rosemary, thyme, or parsley to your onions while cooking to give them a different twist of flavor. You could also deglaze the onion pan with balsamic vinegar or red wine or white wine.

Health Tip:
Meat that is grass-fed, organically raised, and treated humanely has less total fat, saturated fat, cholesterol, and calories. It also has higher ratios of omega-3 fatty acids, which have anti-inflammatory effects on the body and help reduce the risk of heart disease, diabetes, and other chronic diseases.

Sage and pork are a great combination, and you really can't go wrong with however you decide to marry them. Sarah and I featured this recipe last year at the farmers' market and it was a huge hit. The key is to use fresh sage; dried sage just doesn't have the same kick.

-Tanda

THE PERFECT ROAST CHICKEN

INGREDIENTS

1 whole free-range chicken

1 onion

Italian seasoning mix

Sea salt and freshly ground white pepper

Serves 4–6

Discard the giblets (or use in stuffing recipe below) and let the chicken stand at room temperature for about an hour.

Preheat oven to 350°F.

Peel and quarter the onion and stuff into the cavity. Don't bother to close it.

Cover the bird—top to bottom—with a liberal sprinkling of Italian seasoning mix, salt and white pepper.

Place breast side up in a roasting pan. I usually pull the fat off the opening of the cavity and put it on the narrow part of the breast. This both covers and bastes the breast while cooking. I also like to use a rack under the bird, as this gets the skin crispy all the way around—especially if you are using a convection oven.

Cook for about an hour and a half until nice and crispy brown.

Try This:

Add freshly ground nutmeg to the symphony of seasonings. Use fresh herbs from the garden to sprinkle on top. Rub the bird with crushed garlic, or you can make your own stuffing and stuff the bird with an aromatic blend of bread, sage, garlic, and celery.

Health Tip:

Free-range chicken is a great source of omega-3s, an excellent source of protein, and a stock from the bones provides the body with essential minerals.

When living in Oregon, Justin and I would hike up the hill in the rain in December to the farmers' market. We would buy a whole chicken and hike back down the hill, both talking about how we couldn't wait to get it in the oven just so we could enjoy the aromas pouring out of the oven for two hours.

In the winter months, my body, mind, and nostrils crave roast chicken. This smell for me is the equivalent of freshly baked bread; it's home, it's comforting, and it gets my stomach juices going. And, I promise, it's easier than making bread.

-Tanda

CHICKEN ENCHILADAS WITH WINTER SQUASH AND GOAT CHEESE

INGREDIENTS

1 medium butternut squash, peeled and cut into 1-inch cubes, or leftover roasted squash

1½ pounds chicken breasts, or cooked chicken leftovers, or pheasant if available

Organic olive oil

Salt

1 recipe Enchilada Sauce (see page 141), or, in a pinch, a jar of premade enchilada sauce

1 large red pepper, diced

8 ounces herbed chevre goat cheese (optional)

12 GF tortillas (usually brown rice or corn)

Serves 8-10

Preheat oven to 350°F.

Bring pot of water to a boil and cook squash until fork tender, about 20 minutes. Drain, mash, and set aside.

Rub chicken with olive oil and salt, place on a cookie sheet, and bake until meat is just cooked through, about 20–25 minutes.

While chicken is baking and squash is cooking, make enchilada sauce.

When chicken is done, remove from oven and leave the oven on. Let chicken cool until you're able to handle it, then shred meat with hands or two forks into a bowl, add half of the enchilada sauce, and the red pepper; mix.

Evenly spread half of remaining sauce onto bottom of 9x13-inch glass baking dish. Assemble the enchiladas by spreading goat cheese, then mashed squash, then shredded chicken on a tortilla and rolling tightly. Place in dish and repeat. When all enchiladas are assembled, cover them evenly with the remaining sauce and bake in the oven for 30–40 minutes, until edges of tortillas are crispy and brown.

Try This:

As pheasants are runners, not fliers, many people only save the breast meat for cooking. I have discovered to get the most meat out of your pheasant, boil the thighs and breasts with the bones in until just cooked through, about 10 minutes. Set aside until cool enough to handle and debone with a fork. Freeze in zip-top bags for later grab-and-go use.

Health Tip:

Winter squash is full of antioxidants and vitamins and a great source of nutrient-packed carbohydrates. It also makes great leftovers.

The first time I made this recipe was actually in an attempt to use up leftover roasted squash and roast chicken from a previous night's dinner. I have made it all from scratch before, and I'll warn you it can be a bit labor intensive. This recipe is a great option for pheasant if you happen to have a bird hunter in the family (see tip for pheasant above).

-Sarah

SIMPLE BARBECUED CHICKEN

INGREDIENTS

1 organic free-range
(or, even better,
pasture-raised) chicken

Sea salt

Freshly ground
white pepper

Italian seasoning

Serves 4–6

Cut the chicken into thighs, legs, wings, and breasts. Sprinkle liberally with sea salt, white pepper, and Italian seasoning. Grill over medium-high heat until done, about 20 minutes.

Try This:

Try adding fresh herbs or rubbing each piece of chicken with crushed garlic. You can even baste the chicken while it's cooking with white wine and herbs. Serve with corn on the cob (see page 103) and a Rainbow Salad (see page 163).

Health Tip:

Pasture-raised chickens allowed to wander in pasture grass and eat insects have higher levels of beta-carotene than traditionally raised chickens. This will result in their fat being more yellow than white. The first time I saw this I thought something was wrong until I realized the yellow color was increased nutrients.

The smell of barbecued chicken takes me back to standing in our front yard watching my dad over the grill, in his shorts and bare feet, wafting the smoke towards his face to smell the delicious combination of chicken, herbs, maple wood fire, and summer air. The thought brings a smile to my face every time.

-Tanda

ORANGE-CRANBERRY CHICKEN OVER WILD RICE

INGREDIENTS

1 cup wild rice

3 pounds bone-in chicken thighs (or bone-in pheasant breasts and thighs if available)

2 tablespoons organic olive oil

1 large yellow onion, diced

3 large carrots, diced

4 stalks celery, sliced

2 tablespoons fresh ginger, minced

Orange juice, enough to cover chicken and veggies halfway

¼ cup tamari

Dried cranberries

Serves 4

Add 3 cups of water to a saucepan and bring to a boil; add rice, cover, and turn down to low. Let rice cook until kernels puff open, about 45–50 minutes.

While rice is cooking, brown chicken in oil in a lightly greased pan over medium-high heat. Add onion, carrots, celery, and ginger, and cook 3 additional minutes. Add orange juice and tamari to the chicken and veggies, partially cover, and turn down to a simmer for about 15 or 20 minutes until chicken is cooked through. Remove chicken and veggies with a slotted spoon, place onto serving platter, and cover with foil.

Add cranberries to the remaining pan juices and bring to a fast simmer. Reduce liquid by half and place sauce into a serving container or bowl. Serve chicken and veggies over rice topped with sauce and enjoy. Buen Provecho!

Try This:
Add cashews instead of cranberries for a nuttier version. As mentioned above, this recipe easily feeds a crowd, and on a relatively small budget. Tanda and I made this recipe, plus a side of steamed broccoli, for a crowd of thirty, purchasing every ingredient, for just over a dollar a serving. And they had leftovers!

Health Tip:
Wild rice, brown rice, white rice, quinoa, amaranth, and gluten-free oats are all great options for gluten-free grain-based side dishes. Cook them in homemade bone broth or chicken stock for extra nutrients.

In my life before med school, I was a whitewater raft-trip guide for five years. This recipe is my adaptation of a dinner we would make every first night of the five-day trip on the Lower Salmon River. I started making this recipe even more when I discovered how good it is with pheasant instead of chicken. It is a great crowd pleaser and easy to make for thirty-plus people.

-Sarah

CHICKEN SALAD

INGREDIENTS

Leftover roasted or barbecued chicken, chopped
into chunks

1 16 ounce bag of frozen
peas

1 handful fresh dill or parsley, roughly chopped

5–6 dill pickles, finely
chopped

1 bunch scallions, chopped

½ cup organic mayonnaise

Sea salt
and freshly ground
black pepper to taste

Serves 6-8

Put all ingredients in a bowl, stir, and serve.

Try This:

You can add chopped celery, red onion, and even add some paprika for color
and a sweet smoky flavor.

Health Tip:

Mayonnaise has gotten a bad rap in the past because of its fat content, but as
you now know we need healthy fats in our diet to support proper hormone balance, brain and nerve function, and the fluidity of our cellular membranes (the
true brains of the cell).

Last summer we did a river float on the Madison River with Justin's
parents. We had barbecued chicken the night before and had some
leftovers, so I made this for lunch. We parked the boat on the riverbank
and pulled out our picnic. Sarah took one bite of the chicken salad and
groaned with delight. "What did you put in here?" she asked. I listed the
ingredients and her response makes me giggle now every time I make it.
She cocked her head and said, "I never would think to put chicken and
a pickle together, but this is amazing!"
- **Tanda**

OPEN-FACE CHICKEN SALAD SANDWICH

INGREDIENTS

2 pats of organic butter

2 slices GF bread, toasted

2 leaves of red leaf lettuce

2 slices tomato

Chicken salad
(see opposite page)

Freshly ground
black pepper to taste

Serves 1

Butter the toast and place it on a plate. Lay the leaves of lettuce on one piece of toast first, then the tomato slices, and finally top with a big scoop of chicken salad. Give each a few good grinds of black pepper and serve.

Try This:
Instead of butter, you can spread avocado on the toast. Garnish with dill or chopped parsley.

Health Tip:
In addition to chicken being an excellent source of protein that supports the immune system, balance neurotransmitters and hormone function, chicken also contains the trace mineral selenium, which supports many metabolic pathways that aid thyroid function and immune function, and acts as a detoxifying anti-oxidant.

This is one of Justin's favorites. After a long morning of working on the farm, he gets giddy when I prepare this for him. I often pile on the chicken salad so high it ends up toppling all over the plate. But when he's done, there's not a crumb left.
-Tanda

GRILLED PORK CHOPS WITH APRICOT CHUTNEY

INGREDIENTS

Sea salt and
freshly ground pepper
(white or black)

4 thick-cut bone-in
pork chops

Serves 4

Salt and pepper chops before grilling over medium heat until desired temperature; I prefer mine at 150°F. Please beware the health risks of eating undercooked meats, but I just can't stand tough, dry, overcooked pork.

Plate and top with apricot chutney (see page 137).

Try This:

Serve with blanched green beans and white pepper (recipe on page 112) and a savory salad such as kale with Asian mustard dressing or rainbow salad with balsamic vinaigrette.

Health Tip:

Look for pork that is firm and light pink. If you are buying from the grocery store, avoid packages with lots of liquid in them and ones that appear slimy. You can always check the expiration date, too, before you buy to make sure you're getting the freshest of cuts.

This is another quick and easy dinner that seems fancier than the amount of effort it takes to prepare. Presentation does a lot for making a simple dinner look amazing. Smothering a juicy cut of meat with a colorful sweet or savory sauce does wonders for impressing the crowd.
-Sarah

STEAKS ON THE FIRE WITH CARAMELIZED ONIONS

INGREDIENTS

4 New York strips or your favorite cut of meat (T-bone, tenderloin, sirloin)

Good-quality sea salt

Freshly ground black pepper

Serves 4

Start a charcoal fire, ideally using hardwood lump charcoal rather than the briquettes. When you get the charcoal burning, you can add hardwoods like maple, ash, or apple. Play with the aromas and flavors that these different woods add to the meat.

Liberally season the steaks with salt and pepper and place them on the open grill; depending on their thickness, for rare steaks cook about 5 minutes per side. Remove from fire and let rest for 10 minutes. Serve with caramelized onions (see page 121).

Try This:
Try rubbing the steaks with crushed garlic before grilling, or marinate them before you throw them on the fire. This is a great main dish that pairs well with summer salads, roasted broccoli, or corn on the cob.

Health Tip:
Try not to char your steaks; blackening your meats or veggies increases the carcinogens in your food. A great trick for healthier grilling is to use charcoal and hardwoods like maple and hickory because they burn at lower temperatures and won't burn your food as easily.

The key to this is the charcoal fire. There's nothing complicated here. Really just salt and pepper and an open fire will bring out the best in the meat. A simple summer salad, steak on the fire, and fresh, thick cuts of tomatoes with sea salt…voila! You have dinner for a king.

-Tanda

STEAK TACOS WITH AIOLI SAUCE

INGREDIENTS

Sea salt

2 (8-ounce) grass-fed
or wild game steaks,
the cut of your choice

¼ head green or
red cabbage, shredded

½ bunch cilantro,
coarsely chopped

2 limes, juiced

8 corn tortillas

Serves 4

Salt steaks and grill over medium heat to desired doneness. While steaks are cooking, shred cabbage and place in bowl. Toss cabbage and cilantro in limejuice. Salt the mix to taste. When steaks are properly cooked, let them rest under tented foil for 3–5 minutes and then slice thinly with a sharp knife.

Make aioli sauce (see page 135).

To assemble tacos: Heat tortillas on a dry skillet, one at a time, until soft. Drizzle tortilla with aioli, add steak, and top with cabbage mix.

Try This:
Serve with Southwestern salsa as a side (see page 178). If you make extra steak and cabbage, these tacos make a great quick lunch at home.

Health Tip:
This dish is colorful, tasty, and fun, which is the best combination for adding health and healthy food!

This meal is a ton of fun to have with a tableful of friends and a bottle of your favorite red wine. Pass the plate of fixings and assemble the tacos right on your plate over some great conversations.

-Tanda

THAI STEAK SALAD WITH RICE NOODLES

INGREDIENTS

1 box rice linguini

Olive oil

Salt

1½ pounds of
free-range, grass-fed steak

2 large carrots,
peeled into ribbons

1 red pepper,
sliced into rounds

1 cucumber, cut into
quarters, seeded, and
thinly sliced into strips

1 jalapeno, sliced,
seeded for less heat

½ head romaine lettuce,
thinly shredded

½ cup cilantro,
coarsely chopped

½ cup mint,
coarsely chopped

Serves 2-4
Depending on leftovers

Cook rice pasta as directed on the package. Drain, run under very cold water until cool, toss in olive oil, and set aside in a bowl in fridge.

Salt then grill steaks to desired temperature. Let rest 3–5 minutes tented with foil. Then slice as thinly as possible, the key being a very sharp knife.

Prep all veggies and fresh herbs, arranging them on a large platter as you go. Set platter, bowl of pasta, sliced steak, and dressing on table.

Let family or guests arrange their own salad on each plate by placing cold pasta down first, then piling on desired veggies, steak, and herbs, then topping with Thai ginger vinaigrette (see page 165), omitting the cilantro, mint, and chili from the dressing; you can add them on top of the salad separately. Be sure to include a spoon with dressing to be able to get at the delicious, health-boosting garlic and ginger.

Try This:

This recipe easily transforms into the Vietnamese beef noodle soup phó (see page 159).

Health Tip:

It is so important to add raw fresh herbs like ginger, garlic, mint, basil, and cilantro into your food routine. These "spices" are truly nature's medicine. And eating them raw preserves the most of the healing properties.

This salad is a dinner favorite and makes great leftovers. I made this one time for my parents, and my dad saw the pile of ginger and garlic taking up half the cutting board and remarked with surprise, "You're not going to use all of that are you?" With a grin ear to ear, I replied, "Why, yes. Raw!" He was shocked how great the dressing tasted and would never have guessed there was a bucket load of raw garlic and ginger in it if he hadn't seen it with his own eyes.

-Sarah

GOURMET BURGERS STUFFED WITH GOAT CHEESE

INGREDIENTS

1 pound organic ground meat (venison, bison, beef, elk, or antelope)

2 large cloves of garlic, chopped

1/3 cup chopped onion

¼ cup red wine

1 tablespoon sea salt

2 teaspoons freshly ground black pepper

4 tablespoons goat cheese

Serves 4

Heat grill pan over medium heat.

Put everything in a bowl except the goat cheese, and mix with your hands. Form into 4 patties and then press 1 tablespoon of the goat cheese in the center of each burger, covering the cheese with burger. Place on grill and cook each side 2–3 minutes, depending on desired doneness.

Try This:
A great way for family and friends to enjoy these burgers is to create a "burger bar" where you have different toppings, such as mayo, mustard, caramelized onions, sautéed mushrooms, avocado, tomatoes, lettuce, salsa, hot peppers, relish, and any other creative toppings that you can come up with.

Health Tip:
Living in Montana with a husband that hunts, it's easy for me to have access to really healthy meats that are rich in omega-3s. It you don't have access to this, you can find pasture-finished meats in some grocery stores, or get bison when available; your cardiovascular system will thank you.

I was watching the Food Network when this recipe was inspired. I grabbed a pound of ground meat out of the freezer, went out to the garden and picked an onion, popped open a bottle of merlot, and I was off. My husband came home and asked what all the excitement was about, and I just said with a smile, "Wait 'til dinner." This easy recipe takes burgers to another level.

-Tanda

GLUTEN-FREE STUFFED PEPPERS WITH TAHINI

INGREDIENTS

4 red bell peppers, halved lengthwise and seeded

1 pound organic free-range ground beef or wild game

1 tablespoon olive oil

1 large onion, diced

½ head of garlic, minced

1 tablespoon paprika

1 teaspoon cumin

½ teaspoon cayenne

1 teaspoon sea salt

2 carrots, shredded

½ pound crimini mushrooms, chopped

1 (8-ounce) jar sun-dried tomatoes

½ bunch cilantro, minced, plus a few sprigs for garnishes

Optional parmesan cheese, if you tolerate dairy

1 recipe tahini (see page 140)

Serves 4

Preheat oven to 350°F.

Place pepper halves skin side up in large glass baking dish side by side. Cover in foil and place in hot oven.

Heat skillet to medium heat and add 1 tablespoon olive oil. Brown meat for 2–4 minutes. Add the onion and garlic and sauté for 2 minutes more. Then add spices, including salt, and continue to cook until meat is cooked through.

Mix meat, carrots, mushrooms, sun-dried tomatoes, and minced cilantro in a mixing bowl until well combined.

Remove peppers from oven, uncover, turn over with tongs, and stuff with meat and veggie filling. Return peppers to the oven, uncovered, and bake for about an hour. If adding the optional parmesan cheese, do so before returning peppers to oven.

Serve over quinoa (see page 128), drizzle peppers with tahini, and garnish with sprigs of cilantro.

Try This:

Bake any extra stuffing in smaller baking dish on the side; it makes a great lunch for the week.

Health Tip:

Red bell peppers are a great way to get antioxidant vitamins A and C. Peppers are ripe and crisp and fresh in the summer months, so look for them at your local farmers' market or co-op; they are so much tastier fresh off the vine and worth the wait.

When I was in college at the University of New Hampshire, one of my fondest food memories was this funky gyro stand inside a Laundromat on Main Street. Determined to recreate the experience, less the wheat and dairy, I created this Middle-Eastern-inspired dish while reminiscing about this late-night snack spot. I did my best to recreate the experience, thinking of their falafel wrap with homemade tahini, and skipping the infusion of detergent.

-Sarah

GLUTEN-FREE MEAT LOAF WITH DIJON MUSTARD GLAZE

INGREDIENTS

2 tablespoons organic butter

1 medium onion, diced

1 red bell pepper, diced

4 cloves garlic, minced

1 teaspoon thyme

1 teaspoon sea salt

4–5 grinds of freshly ground black pepper

2 pounds free-range ground beef, lamb, or wild game

1 pound andouille sausage, cut into ½-inch pieces

2 farm-fresh eggs, lightly beaten

1 cup cooked quinoa (cook like rice, 2:1 water-to-quinoa ratio)

Serves 6

Glaze

½ cup Dijon mustard 1 tablespoon horseradish ½ cup real maple syrup

Preheat oven to 350°F.

Heat butter in skillet over medium heat. Sauté onion until it begins to soften and then add diced bell pepper, garlic, thyme, salt, and pepper. Cook until peppers are tender (about 5 minutes).

In a large mixing bowl, combine ground meat, andouille, eggs, and quinoa. Add the onion/pepper mixture and mix well.

Combine glaze ingredients with whisk.

Pat meat into a loaf pan. Bake for 30 minutes, then remove from oven and top with glaze. Return loaf to oven and continue baking 10–15 minutes more or until the internal temperature reaches 150°F.

Try This:

Instead of quinoa, you can also use cooked rice or GF bread crumbs made from crumbled GF crackers, GF bread flour mix (about 3 tablespoons), or frozen GF waffles crumbed in a food processor or blender.

Health Tip:

Grass-fed red meats have the same omega-3 content as deep-sea ocean fish. They also contain many essential fat-soluble vitamins such as A, D, E, and K. In Montana and other land-locked states, sourcing beef locally is a much better choice for the environment as well.

This dish was inspired by a recipe I first discovered in *The Complete Meat Cookbook*, by Bruce Aidells and Denis Kelly. This book was a huge stepping stone into my new life as an omnivore after being a born and raised vegetarian for twenty-five years. Interestingly enough, it was given to me at my first meat-eating Christmas by the very woman who cooked me tofu loaf for eighteen years, my mom. This book became my bible to demystify the world of all things meaty and delicious.

-Sarah

DRUNKEN TURKEY

Serves 10
with leftovers

INGREDIENTS

15-pound all-natural, free-range turkey, giblets and neck removed, turkey rinsed and patted dry

2 bottles favorite dry red wine (one for the turkey and one for the toasts)

½ c Cajun seasoning (ideally gluten-free & organic)

¼ c Organic Tamari

1 green apple, cut into large chunks

1 red apple, cut into large chunks

1 orange, quartered

2 lemons, quartered

1 new potato, cut into large chunks

1 russet potato, cut into large chunks

1 sweet potato, cut into large chunks

1 yellow onion, quartered*

3 large shallots, leave whole*

2 heads garlic, separated into cloves*

1 small bunch red grapes, separate from vine

6–8 pats organic butter

*No need to peel these, all will be discarded after making bone broth

Preheat oven to 350°F.

Rinse the inside of turkey with a splash of wine. Combine all fruits and veggies in large bowl and toss to mix. Stuff turkey with fruits and veggie mix. Set aside the extras.

Starting at the neck end, carefully slide hand between skin and breast meat to loosen skin. Evenly distribute pats of butter over the breast meat and under the skin. Tuck wing tips under; tie legs together to hold shape. Place turkey on a rack set in a large roasting pan. Put Cajun seasoning in small bowl and add enough tamari to make it into a paste. Rub paste over turkey. Cover breast area of turkey only with sheet of heavy-duty foil. Scatter remaining fruit and veggie mix in the pan around the turkey.

Roast turkey 30 minutes; baste with ½ cup wine (don't forget the toast!). Continue roasting turkey for 1½ hours, basting with ½ cup wine every 30 minutes. Remove foil from over turkey breast. After removing foil, continue to roast turkey until golden brown and a thermometer inserted into thickest part of thigh registers 180°F (about another hour), continuing to baste with pan juices every 20 minutes. Transfer turkey to platter, tent loosely with foil, and let stand 20 minutes.

Serve, enjoy, and give thanks!

Try This:

This recipe makes an amazing, rich, and spicy bone broth (see page 148). It is my tradition to use this broth to make a post-Thanksgiving, gluten-free turkey noodle soup (see page 149).

Health Tip:

Tryptophan, an amino acid found in turkey, among other things, is famous for making you sleepy, but there is more to the story of this amazing amino. First off, there isn't any more tryptophan in turkey than in other meats. The post-meal drowsiness of Thanksgiving may very well be due to other components of the day. That being said, tryptophan is an essential building block to make the mood-enhancing neurotransmitter serotonin. Before the discovery of Prozac, tryptophan was the favorite treatment for depression in the 1970s, and early trials actually suggest that it is as effective, without side effects, as Prozac is today.

This recipe was inspired by the turkey served for Thanksgiving at the home of a close friend of my mom's. It made a deep impression on my nineteen-year-old self, as it was my first Thanksgiving away from my own family back East. That, and it is so good.

A few years later, this version was born when I was awarded the privilege of being "head chef" of Thanksgiving dinner at home in Rochester, New York. My two uncles, who have both worked as chefs, said it was the best Thanksgiving turkey they had ever had!

The turkey comes out best if you follow the tradition of making a toast to something you are grateful for every time you baste the turkey.
-Sarah

POT ROAST WITH GLUTEN-FREE GRAVY

INGREDIENTS

1 tablespoon sea salt

3-pound roast of grass-fed beef or wild game (antelope is excellent)

2 quarts bone broth, ideally beef bone broth

Serves 4 with leftovers

Preheat oven to 300°F.

Salt the roast before browning over high heat in a cast iron skillet. Brown on all sides and remove the pan from the heat. Add the bone broth to pan and tightly cover it with tin foil and a tight lid.

Place in oven and bake for 3–4 hours at sea level or 4–5 hours above 5,000 ft. Halfway through cooking, turn pan 180° from its first position to ensure even cooking.

Essentially, with this extended cooking time, you are getting the roast to an internal temperature of 200°F, which is the temperature that the connective tissue will begin to melt. By keeping the roast at 200°F for at least an hour, all the sinew breaks down and you are left with one tender beast. I have even cooked an elk roast for 6 hours, and it was amazing.

After the proper cook time has passed, remove roast from the pan, set aside, and tent with foil.

Make gravy in the original roast pan with drippings (see page 138).

Remove foil from roast and, with two forks, flake meat into long strands, like pulled pork. Top with gravy and enjoy.

Try This:

Serve with roasted root veggies (see page 118) and the rainbow salad (see page 164). To cook the veggies and the roast together, simply put veggies in the pan with the roast 90 minutes before the roast should be done.

Health Tip:

If you can get wild game for this dish it's worth it, not only in taste but in the health benefits. Wild game contains the perfect balance of omega-3s and -6s and is naturally a leaner meat than beef. If you don't have access to wild game, grass-fed beef is wonderful, too.

With my vegetarian roots, the comfort-food factor of pot roast was lost on me until I discovered this recipe. I have to give *Cooks Illustrated* cudos for the technique they discovered accidentally by leaving a roast in the oven an hour too long while working in their test kitchen. This recipe has truly turned nonbelievers into pot roast lovers.

-Sarah

ROASTED LEG OF LAMB

INGREDIENTS

6 cloves of garlic

4–6 sprigs rosemary

1 handful fresh parsley

Juice of 1 lemon

3 tablespoons organic olive oil

1 tablespoon sea salt

2 teaspoons freshly ground pepper

1 (4–6 pound) boneless or semi-boneless leg of pasture-fed lamb

Serves 4-6

Preheat the oven to 425°F.

Place garlic, rosemary, parsley, lemon juice, olive oil, salt and pepper in a food processor and blend. Spread this fresh herb paste all over the outside of the lamb and place in a roasting pan. Let the lamb stand at room temperature for 30 minutes, which allows for the meat to cook evenly.

Place lamb in the oven and cook for 20 minutes, then reduce temperature to 350°F and cook until the internal temperature reads 135°F, about 1½ hours.

Remove from oven, place on a cutting board, and let it rest for 15–20 minutes before cutting. Carve and serve.

Try This:

You can use different herb combinations such as mint, parsley, and rosemary, or rosemary, thyme, and sage. Before you put the lamb in the oven, put a whole sprig of rosemary on top to add spice to the rich aroma.

Health Tip:

Pasture-fed lamb is a great source of protein, vitamin B12, and selenium, which are great for adrenal and thyroid health; it is also high in omega-3 fatty acids, which have powerful anti-inflammatory properties.

This is always a request of my dad from the four of us kids over the holidays. It's rich, flavorful, and not a lot of people think to cook lamb, so it surprises family and friends. Oh, and the smell of the lamb roasting in your oven will draw the neighbors into your house, so beware.

-Tanda

RACK OF LAMB

INGREDIENTS

1 tablespoon olive oil

1 rack of lamb
(about 1½ pounds)

5 cloves garlic,
chopped

4 sprigs rosemary,
chopped

Sea salt

Freshly ground
black pepper

Serves 4

Preheat the oven to 450°F.

Rub the oil all over the rack then sprinkle with the garlic and rosemary, followed liberally with sea salt and freshly ground pepper. Place rack in a roasting pan with the ribs curving down and let stand at room temperature for 30 minutes.

Place in the oven and cook for 20–25 minutes. Remove from the oven, cover with tin foil, and allow it to rest for 15 minutes. Carve and serve.

Try This:

You could try using different herbs, such as parsley, sage, thyme, and mint. You could also try adding things to the mix, such as mustard, balsamic vinegar, or even GF bread crumbs to add a crunchy crust to the outside.

Health Tip:

Pasture-raised lamb is a great way to get zinc and niacin in your diet. Zinc plays a key role in stomach and digestive health, and niacin helps support the adrenal glands and our stress response.

There was a time when I didn't care for lamb, but now I can't imagine my spring menu without it. This is my husband's favorite cut, and we usually save it for a special occasion. In the summer months this is great on the grill, and in the winter it's a wonderfully rich comfort food. Serve with a good merlot or one of Oregon's pinot noirs.
-Tanda

ITALIAN SAUSAGE OVER SPAGHETTI SQUASH

INGREDIENTS

1 large spaghetti squash

1 tablespoon organic olive oil

2 pounds Italian sausage

2 medium red onions

2 green bell peppers

1 (32-ounce) jar favorite tomato sauce, *or, better yet,* a 32-ounce jar of home-canned tomatoes from last summer's harvest

Serves 4 with leftovers

Preheat oven to 350°F.

Slice squash in half and place face down in baking dish with ½ inch water. Bake at 350°F for 40–50 minutes, or until fork easily pokes through skin.

While squash is baking, heat olive oil in large skillet over medium heat. Add sausage to pan and brown. If the sausage is in a casing, let it cook about halfway and then remove from pan and slice. Cooked sausage is easier to slice than raw. Return sausage to pan and add onions and peppers. Continue to cook until sausage is cooked through and peppers are softened but still have a little crunch, about 10 minutes more.

When squash is done, remove from oven and drain water from pan. Using a fork, gently flake out inside of squash into long, noodle like strands. Toss in tomato sauce (squash should be hot enough to heat sauce, but if not, be sure to preheat sauce). Serve, topping squash with sausage, peppers, and onions.

Try This:
This dish can also be served over GF pasta such as rice, corn, or quinoa.

Health Tip:
When you eat starches, it's important to add a good-quality healthy fat to it to slow the spike in blood sugar. When you eat starches by themselves, they cause the blood sugar to rise, but if you add a fat source (butter, nut butters, olive oil, coconut oil, avocados, or, in this case, sausage), it slows the rise and is easier on your body and digestion.

If you are so lucky as to live in a city with an artisan gluten-free bakery, pick up a loaf of freshly made, crusty bread to go with this meal. New Cascaida Bakery was our favorite in Portland, Oregon, during med school. Or, better yet, experiment making your own bread. Getting a big crumb and thick crust on GF bread can be a little tricky, but it is delicious and fun to try and master.

-Sarah

STIR-FRY WITH GLUTEN-FREE PASTA AND PEANUT SAUCE

INGREDIENTS

1 pound GF
linguini pasta
(I use pad
Thai rice noodles)

3-4 glugs organic olive oil

Sea salt

16–20 ounces favorite
meat for stir-fry,
such as steak, chicken,
or pork chops
(this would probably
be good with shrimp,
too, but Sarah is
allergic, so we
never think to cook it)

1 glug sesame oil

1 head broccoli,
cut into florets

½ head cauliflower,
cut into florets

2 large carrots, cut into
sticks ¼x3 inches

1 cup sugar snap
or snow peas

1 red pepper,
julienned

2 glugs tamari

Sesame seeds

Peanut sauce
(see page 134)

*Serves 4
with leftovers*

Put a pot of salted water on high heat for pasta. Cook GF pasta as directed on the package. Drain, rinse in cold water, toss in 1-2 glugs olive oil, and set aside.

Salt and grill meat to desired doneness. Set aside under tented foil to rest.

In a large wok or wide chili pan, heat remaining olive and sesame oils over medium-high heat. Add all vegetables to hot oil and cook, stirring frequently. Add a little water and tamari about halfway through the cooking to lightly steam the veggies. Cook until veggies are al dente or still a little crunchy. Toss in sesame seeds at the end after veggies are finished cooking.

When everything is cooked, add peanut sauce to pasta and stir until well combined.

Try This:

Place pasta, veggies and meat into separate serving bowls and place on table— eat family style, passing serving dishes. Raise a glass of wine and enjoy. Buen Provecho!

Health Tip:

Fast cooking methods like stir-frying preserve more of the nutrients in the vegetables, so the crunchier you like your veggies, the better.

The first few years of medical school, Sarah and I were in a lunch group where each one of us would cook a lunch once a week to share with everyone. The first time Sarah made this, I was stopped in the hallway by one of the other members of our lunch group, and she asked if I had eaten yet. I shook my head no. She looked at me wide eyed and said quickly, "You'd better go now, it's gonna be gone. It's the best thing I've ever tasted." Was it ever!

Since then, it has become one of Justin's favorites and a dish that we use when we entertain large crowds. Normally, a peanut sauce overpowers, but this one is subtler and perfectly balanced to make you want to come back for more…and more.

-Tanda

SESAME ENCRUSTED SALMON

INGREDIENTS

3 tablespoons
sesame seeds

1 bunch scallions

3 tablespoons tamari

1 teaspoon freshly
ground white pepper

2-pound fillet of fresh
wild-caught salmon

Serves 4-6

Preheat oven to 400°F.

In a small skillet over high heat, toast the sesame seeds; you'll know they're done when they start popping and jumping out of the pan. Keep an eye on them because they are easy to burn; and when they are toasted, remove from heat and put them in a small bowl and set aside.

Line a cookie sheet with tin foil, lay the scallions out in a line in the middle of the cookie sheet, and place the fillet on top. Drizzle tamari and sprinkle white pepper over top of the salmon, then coat the top of the salmon with the toasted sesame seeds. Place in the oven for 13–16 minutes. Remove from oven, cut, and serve.

Try This:

Try adding chopped garlic and ginger or sprinkle with fresh cilantro before the fish goes in the oven. Serve this with a side of roasted asparagus or top with an avocado salsa.

Health Tip:

Aside from the salmon's much-touted rich omega-3 content, it also contains high levels of vitamin D, a nutrient that Sarah and I see chronically low in an overwhelming majority of our patients. Vitamin D plays an important role in mood, cognition, and immune function.

Going to school in Portland, Oregon, we had no choice but to gorge ourselves on fresh wild salmon. I would walk to the farmers' market every Saturday and buy a fillet fresh off the line. This recipe was one that I made up at Justin's request. Enjoy.
-Tanda

GLUTEN-FREE SALMON CAKES WITH AIOLI

INGREDIENTS

1 tablespoon of organic
butter for sautéing

¼ cup onion,
finely chopped

1 carrot,
finely chopped

¼ cup bell pepper,
finely chopped
(green, red, or yellow)

2 garlic cloves,
finely chopped

1 pound cooked
wild-caught salmon

1 farm-fresh egg

½ teaspoon sea salt

½ teaspoon mustard

6 grinds of
fresh black pepper

¼ teaspoon paprika

A few dashes of
Worcestershire sauce

½ cup gluten-free bread
crumbs
(the small crumbs)

¼ cup organic
mayonnaise

1 tablespoon fresh
parsley, chopped

2- 3 tablespoons organic
butter for frying

Serves 4-6

Sauté the onion, carrot, pepper, and garlic in butter for a few minutes over medium-high heat until soft.

In a bowl, mix the onion, carrot, pepper, and garlic sauté with everything except the salmon and bread crumbs) and stir.

Add in about ¾ of the salmon (reserving some in case your mix turns too dry), and fold in until there is a moist consistency. Begin adding the bread crumbs slowly as you continue to fold. Add slowly because you don't want your cakes to turn out too dry. You should be able to mold the cakes easily, and they should stick together well.

Form into cakes and cool in the fridge for one hour. Remove and fry in butter in a skillet over medium heat. Serve with Basic Aioli. (see page 135)

Try This:

Try using crab in place of the salmon. Serve as an appetizer with an aioli sauce. This is a great way to use leftover salmon from dinner the night before.

Health Tip:

I'm sure you've heard the buzz about salmon's rich omega-3 content. Well, it's true; but it also is a great source of vitamin D, selenium, and vitamin B12.

These are a real crowd pleaser and something that you could do alternatively as an appetizer. The first time I made this, I was on the Oregon coast with my in-laws; it was raining sideways and we couldn't have cared less because of the party going on in our mouths.
-Tanda

RACK OF PORK WITH ROSEMARY
AND GARLIC

INGREDIENTS

1 rack of pork
(3–4 pounds)

4–5 whole cloves garlic

2 tablespoons organic
olive oil, plus extra
to rub on the meat

1–2 cloves of
garlic, chopped

2–3 sprigs of fresh rose-
mary, chopped

Sea salt and freshly
ground black pepper

Serves 8

Preheat oven to 350°F.

Poke 4–5 holes in the skin of the pork with a knife and put a whole clove of garlic in each. Rub the pork with olive oil, and rub with chopped garlic and rosemary. Salt and pepper liberally.

In a large frying pan, heat the 2 tablespoons of olive oil on high, and sear each side of the rack of pork 3–4 minutes each. Remove rack from pan and place in a roasting dish. Put in the oven for about an hour (20 minutes per pound) or until the internal temperature reads 150°F. Remove from the oven and let rest under foil for at least 15 minutes before carving.

Try This:

Serve with roasted veggies, or roasted shallots. Instead of the rosemary, try different herbs, such as sage, parsley, or thyme. Try this with the Rosemary Balsamic Glaze (see page 136) and your guests will be licking their plates.

Health Tip:

Pork from a healthy source is a great source of protein. We love Amaltheia Organic Dairy here in Belgrade, Montana, which does organic pork (as well as goat cheese). But you can find these wonderful, healthful meats in your area at www.localharvest.com or your local farmers' market.

Last winter I was walking around the local grocery store and I saw this cut of meat. You don't see rack of pork very often and it's not expensive, so I bought it. I made it that night for four of us, and after dinner we couldn't stop raving about the meal. I went back to the store the next day, bought them out of the cut, put them in my freezer, and used them for monthly dinner parties all winter long. It's a fun cut of meat to present on a large platter surrounded with roasted root veggies or glazed shallots, and a sprig of rosemary on top.

-Tanda

GRILLED MAHI-MAHI WITH PINEAPPLE CUCUMBER SALSA

INGREDIENTS

2 mahi-mahi fillets,
or tuna steaks

1 recipe pineapple
cucumber salsa
(see page 180)

Serves 2

Grill fish on hot grill pan over medium-high heat for 6 minutes per side for a 1-inch fillet or until fish is firm and opaque. Top with salsa. Serve and enjoy.

Try This:

This recipe pairs perfectly with a green salad with creamy orange dressing (see page 168)

Health Tip:

The health merits of fish are many and relatively well known, especially their omega-3 fat content. But how much fish is enough to get your dose of omega-3s? If you have access to healthy, nontoxic, well-raised wild fish, you can go nuts, four or five times a week (more than enough to be able to skip your fish oil supplement). However, if you don't have God's fish tank in your backyard and happen to live in a land-locked state like Montana, get your omega-3s from local grass-fed, free-range beef instead. Grass-fed beef, bison, and wild game have comparable omega-3 levels as deep-sea, cold-water fish!

It just doesn't get any easier than this—grill fish, top with salsa, quick-dress a side salad, and you have a delicious dinner in, literally, minutes.
-Sarah

WALLEYE IN LEMON BUTTER

INGREDIENTS

2 tablespoons of organic olive oil

10–12 ounces fresh walleye, or other mild white fish

1 large lemon

4 tablespoon organic butter

1 teaspoon sea salt

Serves 2

Pan-fry fish in a well-oiled pan until it just turns opaque and flaky. Juice lemon and add together with butter and salt in a small sauce pan over medium heat until butter is melted. Transfer lemon butter to a small dish and serve on the table with fish. Dip bites of fish into lemon butter as you eat, enjoying every morsel!

Try This:

This recipe goes great with roasted asparagus (page 109) and tarragon salad (page 171) or, for an even more decadent experience, serve with steamed artichokes with lemon caper butter (page 187).

Health Tip:

Butter really is better. Butter is rich in short- and medium-chain fatty acids, which are essential for efficient energy and the health of our nerves and brain. It also is a healthy source of fat-soluble vitamins A, D, and E. Like meat, pasture-raised, grass-fed cows also produce the healthiest butter. Look for pasture butter in your natural foods section of your grocery store, or you can buy it in bulk online (see resources page 200).

Tanda and I are huge fans of eating local meats and produce, and, as such, do not feast on a whole lot of fish, as you may imagine living in Montana. However, a very good friend of ours brought us some fresh-caught walleye from Hauser Lake, about an hour and half north of Bozeman. In my opinion, the only thing to do with any fresh fish is dip it in lemon and butter and let the natural flavors do all the talking.
-Sarah

VEGETABLE SIDES

At our clinic, Clearwater Healthcare, we recommend every person eat at least 5–6 cups of vegetables a day to support his or her health. This often leads to some questions about how best to do that and what our favorite ways to prepare veggies are. So here you go. Welcome to our world of veggies.—Sarah

Raw—See salad section, page

Raw is a great way to eat fresh vegetables. We choose to eat with the seasons, meaning we eat more raw veggies in the summer and early fall and less in the winter and early spring.

How To: Just eat them!

Tip: Mix up how you cut your veggies to experiment with different textures. Shred, slice, dice, slice at a diagonal, use a veggie peeler, puree, etc. Shredded carrots, cabbage, beets, and zucchini are great to add to leafy salads or stand alone as slaw.

Roasting

Our number one favorite way to cook veggies. You can you tell by how many roasting recipes we included. Roasting naturally brings out the sugars in vegetables and makes them delicious. Best for root veggies, squash, and hearty veggies like beets, parsnips, yams, sweet potatoes, sunchokes (Jerusalem artichokes), rutabagas, turnips, carrots, acorn squash, Delicata squash, pumpkins, butternut squash, asparagus, broccoli, cauliflower, brussels sprouts, mushrooms, onion, garlic, fennel, etc.—Sarah

How To: Toss veggies in salt, pepper, and olive oil and roast at 400 degrees for about an hour. Also add fresh herbs such as parsley, sage, rosemary, and thyme to spice things up.

Tip: Treat yourself by topping roasted squash with maple syrup and cinnamon, bacon, or a slice of sharp cheddar cheese (trust us, it's heavenly).

Steamed or Boiled

Best for broccoli, asparagus, cabbage, cauliflower, carrots, green beans, brussels sprouts, celery, or dark leafy greens such as kale, collards, cabbage, bok choy, and Swiss chard.

How To: Place steamer in large pot. Add 1 inch of water and bring to a boil. Add veggies and steam 3–5 minutes until lightly cooked but still crunchy. Avoid cooking these veggies too long as they release sulfur gas and the long cooking time makes them more bitter and mushy. Broccoli is actually sweeter the less you steam it.

Tip: Top steamed veggies with goat cheese, mayo, vinegar, butter, or lemon juice. Also steam with fresh aromatic herbs such as tarragon and mint for a wonderful fresh flavor.

Mashed or Pureed

Best for root veggies and winter squash like beets, parsnips, yams, sweet potatoes, sunchokes, rutabagas, turnips, carrots, and winter squash, including acorn, Delicata, pumpkin, and butternut.

See pureed veggies in appetizer section (page 182-183).

How To: Chop veggies into roughly 1-inch cubes. Cook in boiling water until soft. If mashing squash, be sure to peel before or after cooking, before mashing. Drain water and add salt and butter to taste, then mash with potato masher or bottom of a pint glass, or puree with a hand blender. Also good with a soft goat cheese like chevre.

Tip: To test for doneness, remove one cube from water and place on cutting board. If it easily breaks apart when you apply pressure with a fork, it's done.

Sautéed and Stir-Fried

Best veggies are the same as for steaming. Best for broccoli, asparagus, cabbage, cauliflower, carrots, green beans, brussels sprouts, celery, or dark leafy greens such as kale, collards, cabbage, bok choy, and Swiss chard. Add onions, garlic, ginger, or other herbs for flavor.

Also, this is essentially the same technique as carmelizing onions or shallots.

How To: Over medium heat, add 1 glug olive oil or 2 tablespoons butter to fry pan. Cook veggies, stirring frequently, until softened but still crispy. When stir-frying you can add a splash or two of water and/or tamari to quickly steam/soften veggies.

Tip: Cook veggies in order from hardest to softest, adding greens and mushrooms last. Precooked/leftover root veggies can also be added to stir-fries or sautés near the end to reheat.

Grilled Veggies

Best for slightly hearty veggies, such as asparagus, broccoli, cauliflower, fennel, zucchini, summer squash, peppers, green beans, eggplant, tomatoes, mushrooms, and onions. You can grill root veggies such as carrots, sweet potatoes, and parsnips, but may want to parboil them beforehand to decrease cooking time on the grill.

There are lots of handy vegetable grilling pans, baskets, and things, or just wrapping them in tin foil can do the trick. Larger thickly sliced veggies can even be laid right on the grill.

Also try grilling fruits such as pineapple, apple, pears, peaches, mangos, and nectarines. When grilling fruit, it is best for them to be slightly underripe.

How To: Cut the veggies into large chunks or strips so they can fit well on the grill. If you have a grill stone, they work amazingly for vegetables. I usually marinate the veggies in basic herbs, balsamic vinegar, olive oil, salt, and pepper. Over medium-high heat, toss veggies on the grill and cook a few minutes each side until veggies are tender and have nice grill marks.

Tip: If you want to coat the veggies in fresh herbs, you may want to do it post grilling. Cut them up, put them in a large bowl, and toss them with oil, vinegar, salt, and pepper. Grill. Then, when you take them off, sprinkle freshly chopped herbs on them, such as basil, tarragon, mint, parsley, or cilantro.

Quick Tips:

- Eat 2 cups of sautéed veggies with eggs in the morning for breakfast to get a head start on your 5 cups a day!

- Chop up all veggies for the week on Sunday for faster mornings.

- Roast a whole 9x13-inch pan of veggies on the weekend for easy, yummy veggies all week.

- Chop and individually bag raw veggies for grab-and-go snacking.

RECIPES

CORN ON THE COB WITH ORGANIC BUTTER

INGREDIENTS

6 ears of corn, shucked

½ stick of organic butter

Sea salt

Freshly ground pepper

Serves 6

Add corn to large pot, and fill with water until the ears are floating. Turn on high. As soon as the water starts boiling, remove corn and place on a platter. Melt butter in microwave and drizzle over corn. Salt and pepper to taste.

Try This:

Try adding herbs to the butter, such as chopped-up chives, cilantro, parsley, or basil.

Health Tip:

Corn is often thought of as a vegetable, but is actually a grain. As such, it is a great source of whole food carbohydrates and B vitamins.

Corn is one of the veggies that, if it's not fresh from the farm in mid-July and August, it's not worth buying. Sweet corn should pop in your mouth and make you giggle with joy when you eat it. This is a super easy way to enjoy a little slice of summer.
-Tanda

PARSNIP FRIES

INGREDIENTS

6 parsnips, cut lengthwise in ½ and then into ½-inch-thick pieces

2–3 tablespoons organic olive oil

Sea salt

Freshly ground black pepper

Serves 4-6

Preheat the oven to 425°F.

Cut up the parsnips and put them in a large mixing bowl. Toss with the olive oil until they are coated and transfer to a cookie sheet. Spread them out evenly, sprinkle liberally with sea salt, and give a few good grinds of the black pepper. Bake for 25–30 minutes or until lightly browned. Flip them halfway through baking to brown both sides. Use tongs to do this; I find it's a bit easier than a spatula.

Try This:

Try using sweet potatoes, yams, or even carrots. You could season them with chili powder, cayenne, or paprika. These make a great side to the gourmet burger with caramelized onions or a grilled steak on the fire.

Health Tip:

Parsnips provide an excellent source of vitamin C, fiber, and folic acid.

Somehow I had never eaten a parsnip until into my adulthood. A great friend of ours made these for a group of us while we were on vacation in medical school. Growing up as a vegetarian, it seems amazing there was any vegetable I had not tried, but this white carrot had escaped me. I was totally floored, not only with how delicious they were, but how easy to make, too.

-Sarah

ROASTED SPRING BEETS WITH GOAT CHEVRE

INGREDIENTS

4 large beets or
6-8 smaller ones

4 tablespoons
organic olive oil

2 tablespoons
balsamic vinegar

Sea salt

Fresh ground
black pepper

8 ounces goat
cheese, crumbled

¼ cup toasted
pine nuts (optional)

Serves 4

Preheat oven to 400°F.

Rub the beets with 2 tablespoons of the olive oil and wrap each separately with tin foil. Place them in the oven and roast for 1 hour or until they are tender.

Remove them from the foil, allow to cool, peel, and cut them into 1-inch pieces. Toss them in the remainder of the olive oil and balsamic. Season with the sea salt and black pepper. Arrange on a plate and sprinkle the goat cheese and pine nuts over top. Serve.

Try This:
Serve them over a bed of greens. Try drizzling with a lemon vinaigrette. Serve alongside barbecued chicken, grilled burgers, or fish. They also make a great appetizer.

Health Tip:
These colorful root veggies are high in vitamins and minerals that help protect against heart disease, diabetes, and cancer, especially of the colon. They are high in foliate and manganese, and their bright purple/red coloring lets you know they are also high in antioxidants.

Beets are one of my favorite veggies. They are sweet, earthy, and add great color to a plate. My dad was an adamant hater of beets after being tortured with them as a child. Then, on one of his visits to Montana, I forgot about his hatred and roasted up a big pan of them and ignorantly served them up. To his surprise, these roasted purple morsels didn't taste anything like the over boiled, canned vegetable he remembered, which is only vaguely reminiscent of a real beet.

Roasting veggies naturally enhances their sweetness and is a great way to introduce a new vegetable to a resistant crowd, like kids.

-Sarah

BAKED WINTER SQUASH

INGREDIENTS

2 winter squashes
(acorn, Delicata,
or butternut),
cut in half and
seeds removed

4 pats of
organic butter

Vermont maple syrup

Cinnamon

Sea salt

Freshly ground pepper

Serves 4-6

Preheat oven to 425°F.

Place the squash flesh side down in a baking dish and fill 1/3 of the way with water. Put in the oven and bake for 30–35 minutes, or until you can stick a fork easily through the skin.

Remove from the oven, drain the water, and flip the squash over. Place 1 pat of butter in each squash half, drizzle with maple syrup, and sprinkle with cinnamon, salt, and pepper, then serve.

Try This:

This is a great side to roasted chicken or even grilled steak. You could even fry some whole sage leaves in butter and put those on top when serving.

Health Tip:

Winter squash is a great source of carbohydrates, antioxidants, and vitamins A and C, which help the immune system. There's no better time to eat them than in the winter months.

This is so simple and such a great comfort food in the winter months. It's one of my favorite side dishes a perfectly roasted chicken. I would come home from work, pop the chicken in the oven, and prep the squash. The two of them cooking together makes the house smell like comfort food heaven. These are some of my husband's favorite smells to come home to, not to mention foods.

-Tanda

SLOW-ROASTED TOMATOES

INGREDIENTS

2 good glugs
organic olive oil

14 medium heirloom,
farm-raised tomatoes,
or whatever you
have available

1 teaspoon sea salt

2–3 glugs
balsamic vinegar

Serves 6-8

Add olive oil to a stainless steel fry pan at least 12 inches wide. Cut tomatoes into quarters and add to pan over medium heat. Stir in salt. Turn heat down when tomatoes are heated through. Slowly simmer over low heat, stirring occasionally, until tomatoes break down and are thick and syrupy, about 2–3 hours. Turn off heat and deglaze the pan with balsamic vinegar.

Try This:

This recipe freezes well or can be kept in the fridge for a spell for later use. In this process, we are essentially caramelizing the sugars in the tomatoes. If you desire a smokier flavor, roast an additional 30 minutes to an hour. Use in soups (see tomato bisque recipe, page 153), to top meats or veggies, or combine with homemade pesto and a few poached eggs and you have a divine breakfast.

Health Tip:

Tomatoes are such a rich source of all things healthy. Lycopene is one of its antioxidants that is touted most, and for good reason. It's a protector of the cardiovascular system and has been shown to help fight and prevent cancer. And if you have the choice, go with organic when you can.

This recipe is a bit long in cook time, but it is very short in prep time. During medical school, part of how I kept myself healthy was to spend my Sundays cooking and studying. I might have had two or three different pots going on the stove and a chicken roasting in the oven all at the same time while I got through microbiology.

-Sarah

ROASTED ASPARAGUS

INGREDIENTS

1 pound of fresh
spring asparagus

Organic olive oil

Sea salt

Freshly ground pepper

Serves 4-6

Preheat oven to 425°F.

Cut the stem ends off of the asparagus and place on a cookie sheet. Drizzle liberally with olive oil and toss until they are all coated. Sprinkle a good amount of sea salt and several grinds of black pepper over them. Place in the oven and cook for 15–20 minutes until the tips get a little crisp and the ends are still tender.

Try This:

You can sprinkle Parmesan on top or even toss the asparagus with some balsamic to add some sweetness. This is a great side with lamb or pork.

Health Tip:

Asparagus is a great food to support the liver. It's high in vitamin K and foliate and full of antioxidants.

I look forward to these plants every spring. The taste of fresh spring asparagus right out of the ground will make you grin in delight. When I worked on my best friend's farm as a teenager, we would wake early in the morning, stand in the dew with our buckets in hand, and fight over who got to go out to the asparagus patch. We were paired up, and the two of us would walk along the rows with our eyes peeled, trying to decipher the green fingerlike shoots from the surrounding weeds. When we would find them, one usually went in the bucket and one in the stomach.

This is a super easy recipe, and it gives these greens a chance to pop with flavor.

-Tanda

ROASTED BROCCOLI AND CAULIFLOWER

INGREDIENTS

1 head of broccoli

½ head of cauliflower

6 tablespoons
organic olive oil

3 tablespoons
white wine vinegar

2 teaspoons sea salt

Several good grinds
of black pepper

1–2 tablespoons of
fennel seeds (optional)

Serves 6

Put a baking sheet in the oven and heat to 500 degrees.

While oven is preheating, cut the stalk off of the head of broccoli, remove skin, and chop in half lengthwise. Roughly chop the heads of broccoli and cauliflower and put in a mixing bowl. Toss with the olive oil, vinegar, salt, pepper, and fennel seeds.

When the oven is heated, remove the baking sheet and place the broccoli and cauliflower on it so they are in rows, not piled on top of each other. Place back in the oven for 10–15 minutes until nicely browned and tender.

Try This:
Serve alongside barbecued chicken or steak with a garden salad. You could chop up some onion and garlic and toss it in with the mix. Instead of the fennel seeds, you could try other spices, such as cumin, or dried herbs.

Health Tip:
Broccoli is full of all sorts of vitamins and minerals, but recent research has pushed this veggie for its anticancer properties. Cauliflower is a wonderful source of vitamin C and contains an enzyme that helps the liver detoxify.

One Sunday afternoon Sarah and I were losing ourselves in her collection of *Cooks Illustrated* magazines. I stumbled upon a recipe where they roasted broccoli. It had never occurred to me to do such a thing. So we tried it that night and fell in love. This is our adapted version and a totally new way of experiencing broccoli and cauliflower. Enjoy!

-Tanda

BLANCHED GREEN BEANS WITH WHITE PEPPER

INGREDIENTS

¾ pound fresh green beans

1 tablespoon organic butter

Sea salt

Freshly ground white pepper

Serves 4

Cut the tips off of the green beans. Place the beans in a sauce pan with a tight-fitting lid, fill halfway with water, place on the stove, and bring to a boil. Cook for 1 minute, remove from heat, and drain water. Add butter, salt, and white pepper, toss, and serve.

Try This:

This is a great side for pork chops, grilled chicken, or fish. You can add toasted sliced almond for a nutty crunch. Try this with fresh tarragon as well.

Health Tip:

The green bean's combination of silicon, vitamin K, calcium, and magnesium makes it a great supporter of bone health. Eat your beans!

I remember standing in my parents' kitchen and watching the water boil over some fresh green beans that we had picked minutes before, and my dad saying that white pepper and green beans were meant to be together. So here ya go.

-Tanda

GARLIC CAULIFLOWER MASHERS

INGREDIENTS

1 head cauliflower, cut into large florets

4 cloves garlic

3 tablespoons organic butter

¼ cup rice milk or coconut milk

Sea salt

Freshly ground pepper

Serves 6

Boil or steam cauliflower until soft, about 10 minutes. Drain well. Add garlic, butter, and rice milk, and puree with a hand blender until smooth. Add salt and pepper to taste.

Try This:

Try purple cauliflower, found at many local farmers' markets. Different-colored vegetables are a great way to get kids excited about tasting them.

Health Tip:

Typical white potatoes are high in starch and calories and low in nutritional value. This is a great alternative to mashed potatoes, providing the complex carbohydrates of cauliflower and none of the joint-pain-inducing chemicals found in nightshade vegetables (which include potatoes, tomatoes, eggplant, bell peppers).

This was another one of those recipes that we got to try in our lunch group in medical school. Potatoes are part of the nightshade family and tend to be inflammatory, so instead, one of our friends decided to smash up some cauliflower, and to all of our surprise it was fantastic.

-Tanda

STEAMED ASPARAGUS WITH FRESH LEMON

INGREDIENTS

1 bunch asparagus, the thinner the stalks, the better

2 pats of organic butter

1 lemon

Sea salt

Freshly ground pepper to taste

Serves 6

You can steam or boil these. Gently snap off the thick end of one stalk. Use this size as a gauge to cut the ends off the rest of the bunch. If you have a tall enough steamer pot, steam asparagus until it turns bright green, about 3–5 minutes. If not, boil asparagus in water for 1 minute.

Place asparagus on platter and melt several pats of butter over it. Squeeze lemon juice and flavor with sea salt and pepper to taste.

Try This:

Try steaming broccoli, cauliflower, or carrots in the same way, simply adding lemon and butter for flavor.

Health Tip:

Steaming vegetables is the healthiest way to cook them, as it preserves the most nutrient value. If you boil them, flash boil them for very short periods of time, such as 1–3 minutes.

This recipe is so good and so easy that people didn't believe there was no marinade when we served it at the Bogart Farmers' Market. Asparagus is one of those veggies that you don't have to do a whole lot to, and it's so much better fresh that when the springtime shoots come into season and into your grocery store, snap them up, eat them like kings, and, when the season is done, thank it and look forward to next year's crop.

-Tanda

MASHED SWEET POTATOES

INGREDIENTS

2 large sweet potatoes

Organic butter

Sea salt to taste

Serves 4

Boil sweet potatoes until fork tender, about 20 minutes, drain, and puree with a hand blender. Add butter and salt to taste and serve piping hot.

Try This:

Substitute any root veggie or winter squash, such as beets, parsnips, yams, sunchokes, rutabagas, turnips, carrots, acorn squash, delicate squash, pumpkins, and butternut squash.

Health Tip:

Where there is color, there are nutrients. Sweet potatoes are a good source of dietary fiber, vitamin B6, and potassium, and a very good source of vitamin A from beta-carotene, vitamin C, and manganese.

Just about every time I make these, someone asks me if I added any maple syrup or brown sugar. I never do. Everyone is always surprised at how sweet sweet potatoes can be all on their own. FYI, they do tend to be sweeter than yams.
-Sarah

SAUTÉED KALE WITH RICOTTA SALATA GOAT CHEESE

INGREDIENTS

2 bunches fresh kale

3 tablespoons organic olive oil

1 large onion, sliced

4–5 cloves garlic, chopped

2 teaspoons tamari

Freshly ground pepper

3 ounces ricotta salata goat cheese

Serves 6

Trim out the large stems of the kale and discard; coarsely chop the greens. Set aside.

Heat the 3 tablespoons of olive oil in a large skillet or wok over medium-high heat. Add the onions and garlic and sauté for 5–6 minutes until they start to get soft. Add the greens, tamari, and pepper. Stir them often until the greens get tender, about 7–10 minutes.

Transfer the cooked greens to a serving plate and crumble the ricotta salata over the top.

Try This:

Add toasted sesame seeds, mango, basil, cilantro, or mint to give the flavors a twist. Combine with grilled white meats, such as pork, chicken, or fish. You could serve with other sautéed veggies or rice for an easy, nutritious meal for the whole family.

Health Tip:

Kale and other dark greens are packed with essential vitamins and minerals, such as vitamins A, C, K, and calcium. They help detoxify the liver and are anti-carcinogenic. So eat your greens!

Kale is one of those vegetables that most people only recognize because it was used as a garnish on their plate the last time they went out for dinner. The truth is, this is so much more than a garnish. It's one of the most nutrient-rich vegetable options and is much easier to add to your diet than you might think. This recipe was one of the earlier ones we tested at the farmers' market last summer and people were begging for more.

-Tanda

ROASTED ROOT VEGETABLES

INGREDIENTS

2 sweet potatoes, chopped

1 bunch carrots, chopped

1 bunch parsnips, chopped

2 rutabagas, chopped

1 large onion, roughly chopped

4 cloves of garlic, roughly chopped

1/3–1/2 cup organic olive oil

1 cup fresh parsley, sage, rosemary, chopped

Sea salt

Freshly ground black pepper

Serves 4-6

Preheat the oven to 425°F.

In a large bowl toss the veggies and garlic with the olive oil and herbs. Place on a baking sheet or roasting pan and sprinkle liberally with salt and pepper. Roast, stirring occasionally, until the veggies are tender, about 25–30 minutes. Serve.

Try This:

Try this with an array of veggies such as turnips, potatoes, yams, brussels sprouts, even kale. Also you can try splashing some balsamic vinegar in the mix for some jazz of flavor.

Health Tip:

The root veggies are a favorite of mine and remind me of winter months and warm fires. They are also all high in vitamins and minerals, including Bs, potassium, and iron. They are packed with antioxidants and are food for the brain, heart, and skin.

This is a go-to recipe. You can roast a huge pan of them and use for breakfast the next day, or lunch. But watch out, they are so good you might not have leftovers.

-Sarah

SAUTÉED VEGGIE MEDLEY

INGREDIENTS

2 tablespoons organic olive oil or coconut oil

2 cloves garlic, chopped

1 zucchini, julienned

1 summer squash, julienned

2 carrots, julienned

1 bunch scallions with the roots cut off

1 red bell pepper, julienned

Serves 2-4

Heat oil in a wok or large frying pan, add the garlic, and cook for a few minutes; watch not to burn it. Then add the vegetables and sauté veggies until tender, about 10 minutes. Remove from heat and serve.

Try This:

Get creative with this! You can try different combinations of vegetables with different herbs. Try fingerling potatoes with cherry tomatoes and thyme or green beans, red cabbage, onions, and cauliflower with basil or parsley.

Health Tip:

Where do I begin? So much is in here—vitamins, minerals, antioxidants, healthy fats, etc. A professor in school said, "Eat the rainbow; it's the best multivitamin there is."

This is a quick and easy way to get fresh veggies on your plate, and it's fun to watch the combinations of vegetables change with the seasons and light up your palate. It makes a great side to grilled steak or chicken.

-Sarah

CARAMELIZED ONIONS

INGREDIENTS

1 tablespoon
organic butter

2 red or yellow
onions, sliced

Sea salt

Freshly ground
black pepper

2 tablespoons
balsamic vinegar

Serves 2-4

Heat the butter in a skillet with a tight-fitting lid over high heat. Add the onions and stir occasionally for 3–4 minutes. You actually want them to brown a bit because it brings out the sugar in the onion. Add the salt, pepper, and balsamic. After 3–4 minutes on high, reduce the heat to low, cover, and let simmer for 10–15 minutes, stirring occasionally. Serve.

Try This:

Instead of the balsamic, you can try red or white wine. Also try adding herbs, such as thyme or rosemary. Serve this over steak, burgers, or pork.

Health Tip:

Lots of studies have been done showing the cardiovascular benefits of onions and garlic. They are also antimicrobial and contain anticancer properties.

Last winter I was at a baby shower and the host had made sliders with caramelized onions that were to die for. I asked her what she did to make them that way. She quickly rattled off a few things, which in the fury of running around trying to make the mother-to-be happy, I never did write down. I then came home and made my own version.

-Tanda

GRILLED ZUCCHINI AND SUMMER SQUASH WITH TARRAGON

INGREDIENTS

3 fresh zucchinis,
sliced thin lengthwise

3 fresh summer squash,
sliced thin lengthwise

2 cloves garlic,
minced

3 tablespoons
organic
olive oil

Sea salt

Freshly ground
black pepper

1 handful of fresh
tarragon, chopped

Serves 4

Heat grill or grill pan to medium-high heat.

Toss the zucchini and summer squash and garlic in 2 tablespoons of olive oil and season liberally with salt and pepper. Grill the zucchini and squash until they're tender and have brown grill marks, about 3–5 minutes each side. Remove from the grill and toss with the remaining 1 tablespoon of olive oil and the tarragon. Serve immediately.

Try This:

Serve alongside grilled chicken, steak, or lamb. Try adding other veggies or herbs, such as parsley, cilantro, thyme, or eggplant, potatoes, and yams. You can sauté this dish as well to give it a different flavor. You can also add a splash of red or white wine vinegar to give it a kick.

Healtth Tip:

Zucchini and summer squash are particularly high in manganese and vitamin C. Studies have shown them to be helpful in men's health and a protector of the heart and vascular systems.

Zucchini and summer squash are a great way to add color to your plate, and the combination of tarragon makes this dish unique and so satisfying. I had a tarragon plant last summer in one of our planters on the front porch. It grew like mad, so I was putting it in and on everything. This recipe was inspired, then, by last year's tarragon explosion.

- Tanda

BALSAMIC GLAZED ROASTED SHALLOTS

INGREDIENTS

5–6 shallots,
chopped in ½

2 tablespoons
organic olive oil

2 tablespoons
balsamic vinegar

Sea salt

Freshly ground pepper

Serves 4

Preheat the oven to 425°F.

In a bowl, toss the shallots with the oil, vinegar, salt, and pepper, place in a roasting pan, and roast for about 40 minutes or until golden brown, as it depends on the size of the shallots.

Try This:

Try adding herbs to change up the flavor, such as rosemary, thyme, sage, or parsley.

Health Tip:

Shallots, part of the Allium family, are full of healthy goodness. Really, there's nothing that these guys can't do. They support heart health, bone, and connective tissue; they are anti-inflammatory, antimicrobial, and anticancer. So load up!

Shallots are sweeter than onions and have the most wonderful flavor. I made this recipe up one day while I was roasting a rack of pork in the oven. I got this image of serving the pork surrounded by beautiful glazed shallots. So I did. And this is what I came up with.

-Tanda

GLUTEN-FREE GRAINS

There are several wonderful gluten-free grains out there that make great side dishes and additions to a diet rich in veggies and healthy meats. Our favorites are brown rice, wild rice, quinoa, polenta (corn meal), and gluten-free oats. These make great substitutes for bread crumbs in recipes or as a starchy side dish instead of pasta or bread with dinner.

There are some other ancient grains that are gluten free, including amaranth, teff, buckwheat, and millet. These grains tend to be a bit heartier, and I have not found them to useful in my own diet, as I feel better limiting grains in general, but feel free to play with all of the above.

To add essential minerals and many immune-boosting health factors, always cook your grains in bone broth instead of plain water. You can also give your grains a vitamin B boost by adding nutritional yeast. This yellow flaky stuff is a great substitute for the flavor of cheese. I grew up on nutritional yeast as a vegetarian, and while I have tossed out many of my vegetarian culinary traditions, this one has stayed proudly in my pantry.

-Sarah

RECIPES

CREAMY POLENTA

INGREDIENTS

4 cups water
or stock

1 cup medium
ground corn meal

4 tablespoons
organic butter

1/3 cup goat cheese

Sea salt

Freshly ground pepper

Serves 6-8

Bring water to a boil and add corn meal in a thin stream while stirring to prevent lumps. Reduce heat to low. Add remaining ingredients and cook, stirring often, until creamy (about 15 minutes). Salt and pepper to taste.

Try This:

You can try adding other cheeses or fresh herbs to this dish to take it in a different direction. You can also fry the leftovers the next day for breakfast and put a couple of eggs on top.

Health Tip:

Corn meal is a great gluten-free option for those of you who want something other than meat, veggies, and fruit. It's super inexpensive. Look for it in the bulk section of your grocery store.

Growing up, Dad would make polenta on occasion, and we kids loved it. When I got my own kitchen I started playing around with the versatile gluten-free grain. The addition of the goat cheese adds a whole new dimension to the dish. Most of our guests aren't familiar with polenta, and as soon as it hits their taste buds, they are reaching for more.
-Tanda

BASIC QUINOA

INGREDIENTS

1 cup bone broth

1 cup quinoa

Sea salt to taste

Rinse quinoa in cool water and drain. Bring broth to a boil, add quinoa, turn down heat to a simmer, and cover. Cook until quinoa has absorbed all the broth, about 20 minutes. Let rest for 5 minutes, then fluff with a fork. Salt to taste.

Try This:

Add 1 tablespoon curry powder to broth and cook to make curried quinoa. Also, an old throwback from my vegetarian days, add ½ cup nutritional yeast to cooked quinoa for a "cheesy" flavor. Try using quinoa pasta when making Italian dishes.

Health Tip:

Quinoa is a grain relatively high in protein and is also a complete protein, meaning it provides the nine essential amino acids. It is a great source of magnesium, a natural relaxant that helps prevent or relieve headaches and promotes heart health.

I did not discover this ancient grain until I chose a gluten-free lifestyle. Now you can find it everywhere. I love the way the husk curls into a little curly-q when cooked. I always loved little cute things. That's probably why this is my absolute favorite grain. Cook and use it just like you would rice or couscous. It also makes a great breakfast grain; just don't forget your side of protein.

-Sarah

QUINOA MEDITERRANEAN SALAD

INGREDIENTS

4 cups cooked
quinoa, chilled

1 heirloom tomato, diced

1 red onion, diced

1 red bell pepper, diced

1 yellow or orange
bell pepper, diced

1 cucumber,
quartered and sliced

1 (6 ounce) jar pitted
kalamata olives, drained

2–3 glugs organic
olive oil

¼ cup flat leaf
parsley, chopped

Sea salt

Fresh ground
black pepper

Serves 6-8

Combine all ingredients in a large mixing bowl. Add salt and pepper to taste.

Try This:

Add lemon juice to this recipe and you have gluten-free tabouleh.

Health Tip:

When I do make grain based salads, I always try to have half the bulk be veggies to add more nutrients and decrease the faster-burning simple carbohydrates. You still get the experience of a starchy dish without the crash in energy later.

I used to make this as a pasta salad before I went gluten-free. Something about the flavors just says summer to me. It's a great dish to pass at potlucks or summer barbecues. I have made it with gluten-free pasta, but I think my favorite version is with quinoa.
-Sarah

GREEN RICE

INGREDIENTS

1 bunch spinach

1 bunch cilantro

½ bunch flat-leaf parsley

2 jalapeño peppers

1 teaspoon sea salt
2½ cups broth

1 small onion, diced

2 tablespoons organic
olive oil or butter

2 cloves garlic, chopped

1½ cups jasmine rice

4 tablespoons minced
chives, for garnish

Serves 4-6

Blend spinach, cilantro, parsley, peppers, and salt with 1 cup broth to liquefy. In a medium sauce pan, sauté onions, butter, garlic, and rice to soften. Add contents of blender and remaining broth to rice. Bring to a boil, then turn down to a simmer for 15 minutes or until rice is thoroughly cooked. Turn off heat and let rice stand covered another 10 minutes.

Try This:

This dish is a great side with Mexican flavors, such as chicken and squash enchiladas or mole pulled pork (see page 73). Mix in fresh salsa or corn and black beans for a more colorful presentation.

Health Tip:

Wonders of chlorophyll! Chlorophyll has the identical structure to hemoglobin except that it has magnesium instead of iron in the center. It functions very similarly to hemoglobin, supporting energy, oxygen transport, and overall circulation. It is immune boosting, increases circulating red blood cells, cleanses the liver, is antioxidant and anti-cancer, chelates heavy metals, is high in magnesium, and supplies vitamins K and C, folic acid, iron, and calcium.
So eat your greens!

This was another one of those farmers' market hits that caught people off guard. My favorites were the parents who would walk by with their children and the kids would grab the sample cup off the table and devour it. Mom or Dad would look at us and ask, "That was green, and she ate it? I need to know more."
-Tanda

GLUTEN-FREE CORNBREAD STUFFING WITH ANDOUILLE SAUSAGE

INGREDIENTS

1 recipe GF cornbread (Grandma's Unsweetened Cornbread Mix by the Cravings Place)

1 stick organic butter

1 large onion, chopped

2 cups celery, chopped

2 jalapenos, minced (seeded if you desire less heat)

1 quart chicken bone broth

1 pound andouille sausage, crumbled in food processor

1 teaspoon sea salt

5 eggs, beaten well

Serves 6

Prepare the cornbread with the options of maple syrup, butter, and chili flakes (see resources page 200).

Preheat oven to 350°F.

Melt butter in medium fry pan over medium heat. Sauté onion, celery, and jalapenos until onions are translucent, about 7 minutes.

Crumble cornbread into a large mixing bowl. Add sautéed veggies, broth, sausage, salt, and eggs, and combine well. Pour mixture into a greased baking pan and bake until stuffing is cooked through, about 45 minutes.

Try This:
For a faster version, simply add andouille sausage to cornbread batter and bake as directed on package.

Health Tip:
This is a great way to have a gluten-free Thanksgiving. We have passed this on to many of our patients, because when the holidays roll around, nobody wants to feel deprived, and this is one recipe that will become a Thanksgiving tradition and will please all types of eaters.

I made this recipe up just this past year for Thanksgiving. Two good friends were hosting the traditional dinner of thanks with a delicious Southwestern theme. We had a twenty-pound turkey rubbed in chili powder stuffed with onions, peppers, and tomatillos, appetizers of corn salsa and guacamole with chips, sides of this stuffing, red beans and rice, sopapillas, and flan for dessert. A friend from Arizona demanded traditional green bean casserole, so we added it to the mix. We toasted that day with home-made cilantro-lime margaritas. It was a perfect spicy feast to warm our insides while feet of snow fell outside.
-Sarah

SAUCES

Making sauces from scratch is not an act you find many American families doing anymore. However, sauces and dressings are one of the major places we end up eating poorly made, processed foods full of extra sodium and added sugars. The oils used are typically the cheapest variety, not the healthiest ones, and salad dressings especially are a hidden source of sugar.

I think many people think homemade sauces are complicated and take too much time. There are probably a few complicated, time-consuming sauces out there, but not these. All the sauces in this section are relatively quick to make, and all of them can be made in quantity and stored in the fridge or even frozen. The little extra time it takes to make these from scratch adds a huge amount of health to your life, providing the chance to choose healthy ingredients and avoid a lot of preservatives and added salt and sugar.

One summer during college I lived with a biology major who was a bit overzealous with planting basil in our garden. He planted over thirty plants, and we had fresh basil practically coming out of our ears that summer. We would harvest five-gallon-buckets worth of the gorgeous, green leaves and have pesto-making parties that would go on for hours. We would pack the pesto into ice cube trays and freeze it. When the pesto was frozen, we would pop out the cubes and store in zip-top bags. These little nuggets of flavor became perfect single-serving doses for pasta, veggies, and meats all winter long.

-Sarah

RECIPES

PEANUT SAUCE

INGREDIENTS

2 garlic cloves, minced

1 tablespoon
ginger, minced

1 chili pepper
(vary the heat with
more or less chili)

2 tablespoons honey

¼ cup fresh cilantro

Juice of 1 lime

1 tablespoon sesame oil

¼ cup tamari

¼ cup rice wine vinegar

¼ cup smooth
natural peanut butter

Chop first five ingredients in a food processor. Place in a bowl and combine with all remaining ingredients except peanut butter. Stir in peanut butter by hand until sauce is smooth and creamy. Sauce will thicken in the fridge.

Try This:

Add coconut milk to make richer. Use sauce for dipping with chicken or beef satay. Pour over rice noodles and top with stir-fried veggies.

Health Tip:

The ginger, garlic, and chili pepper all contain healing properties for the heart and vascular system and are antimicrobial. Cilantro detoxifies heavy metals from the body and can help with lowering blood sugar.

Note about peanut butter:

Typically, we recommend avoiding peanut butter, as it can be highly inflammatory, but I have tried this recipe with almond butter and it is just not as good. So, all things in moderation, and enjoy this delicious treat!

I probably make this at least every other month in a triple or quadruple batch to keep in the fridge for quicker meals. I have been known to surprise people by returning the sauce to the peanut butter jar. They unsuspectingly think they are getting plain peanut butter, and it's anything but. That would make one heck of a spicy PB&J!

-Sarah

BASIC AIOLI

INGREDIENTS

2 cups organic mayon-
naise

2 cloves garlic

1 teaspoon Dijon mustard

Fresh lemon juice to taste

Sea salt and freshly
ground black pepper

Place all the ingredients in a blender or food processor and blend until smooth.

Try This:

Aioli is a great way to jazz up fish, chicken, or pork, and a true classic with salmon. Spice it up and get creative by adding more lemon juice or basil, cayenne, roasted tomatoes, roasted peppers, even fennel tops or roasted nuts. You can use any herb, really, such as parsley, tarragon, dill, basil, even mint. Play with this one!

Health Tip:

I know mayo gets a bad rap, but it is mostly just eggs, vinegar, mustard, oil, lemon juice, and salt. Get into a habit of making your own and it adds extra pleasure when you smear it on gluten-free bread or make it into a flavorful aioli sauce.

Aioli is a pretty new addition to our kitchen, and it's a great way to wake up chicken and pork, and it's made for fish.
-Tanda

ROSEMARY BALSAMIC GLAZE

INGREDIENTS

½ cup real maple syrup

¼ cup balsamic vinegar

¼ cup dijon mustard

1 tablespoon tamari

1 tablespoon
organic butter

2 tablespoons fresh
rosemary, chopped

Several grinds of
fresh black pepper

Mix the maple syrup, vinegar, mustard, and tamari in a bowl and set aside. In a saucepan over medium high heat, add the butter and cook until bubbling, then add the bowl of ingredients. Bring to a boil; add the rosemary and the pepper. Constantly stir the glaze until it reduces by about a third or you can run a spatula through it and it takes several seconds for it to reform to fill the bottom of the pan.

Try This:

Try adding other herbs to replace the rosemary, such as sage or thyme. Pour this over wild-caught salmon or halibut, grass-fed organic pork, or lamb.

Health Tip:

Making your own sauces is a great, easy way to add a ton of health to your life. Processed sauces typically are full of many unhealthy, unwanted ingredients. By making your own, you get to choose the best quality oils, sweeteners, and spices possible. Rosemary is known to improve memory, support the nervous system, relieve stomach upset, and lift the mood to improve depression.

This was another one inspired by the food channel. I was studying for an exam with a cooking show in the background and got distracted when they said "maple syrup." I closed my anatomy book and started jotting down some notes. That night I made my own version and poured it over grilled pork chops. I thought Justin was going to eat his plate.

-Tanda

APRICOT CHUTNEY

INGREDIENTS

2 tablespoons organic butter

1-inch thumb fresh ginger, grated

1 medium sweet onion, diced

2 cups dried apricots, coarsely chopped

1 cup dried cherries (or substitute cranberries)

1 cup water

½ cup sweet white wine

¼ cup real maple syrup

Zest of ½ organic orange, juiced

½ teaspoon sea salt

Melt butter over medium-low heat. Add ginger and onion and sauté until onion is soft. Add apricots and cherries and continue to sauté 2 minutes more. Add all liquid ingredients, zest, and salt. Bring to a slow simmer and reduce by half.

Try This:

Use fresh fruit if in season. Try peaches instead of apricots, and cranberries or currents instead of cherries.

Health Tip:

Generally speaking, fresh whole fruit is the best choice for our health. Usually one can easily eat far more dried fruit than one would if it were whole. The issue is that dried fruit has a higher concentration of sugar in it than whole fruit. That being said, for cooking, using a limited amount of rehydrated dried fruit is a power-packed flavor option.

When we lived in Portland, Justin would take our Labrador out and bird hunt in the wee hours of the morning in the fall when the weather was raining and cold. He would come home soaked to the bone but happy as a clam, with his hands gripped around the tails of ducks and pheasants.

I struggled for a while as to how to cook them and make them delicious. But Sarah came up with this to go with the pheasants and it's just divine. You can also use this with pork, chicken, or duck.

-Tanda

GLUTEN-FREE GRAVY

INGREDIENTS

At least 4 cups
bone broth or liquid
from braising a pot roast

3 tablespoons rice flour
or other GF flour you
have on hand
(see resources page 200)

3 tablespoons
organic butter

Add bone broth to a sauce pan over medium-high heat. Reduce the liquid by half. While liquid is reducing, put GF flour into a 2-cup liquid measuring cup and slowly whisk in a stream of cold water until flour becomes a thin paste.

When liquid in the pan has reduced to the desired amount, turn down the heat to medium and add butter. When the butter is melted, add the flour paste by whisking into the liquid in the pan. Continue to stir with a whisk over medium heat until it's thick. Season with additional salt and pepper if desired.

Try this:

If you are making gravy to accompany a roast or braised meat, use the pan the meat was cooked in to make the gravy, letting the pan drippings flavor the gravy. The flavor from gravies made this way is incredible.

Health tip:

Gravy has had a place at our tables for a long time as an unhealthy food. Truthfully, using pasture-raised or organic butter and gluten-free flour makes this an essential healthy-fat food in your repertoire. Just because gravy is high in calories doesn't make it an unhealthy food in moderation.

It never occurred to me to make gravy with rice flour until I chose to avoid gluten in my diet; however, I swear it is the best thickening agent I have ever found. Even friends who still eat wheat and dairy have been converted to avid users of rice flour and other gluten-free flours to thicken their sauces.

-Sarah

TAHINI

INGREDIENTS

1 cup raw sesame seeds

¼ cup organic olive oil

2 lemons, juiced

Zest of ½ organic lemon

1 teaspoon sea salt,
plus more to taste

Water

Toast seeds in a dry pan over medium-high heat until they being to pop like popcorn. Transfer to food processor and pulse until finely ground (the finer the better for a smooth sauce). Slowly drizzle olive oil, then lemon juice and zest, into food processor while continuing to blend. Add salt. Add a little water if needed for desired consistency. Add additional salt to taste.

Try This:

This sauce is great over veggies and eggs in the morning or with GF whole grains, such as quinoa or brown rice.

Health Tip:

Sesame seeds contain essential fatty acids that support the production of progesterone in the body. Tahini is a great variation to get these nutrients into your diet on a regular basis. When eating any seeds such as sesame, flax, sunflower, or even pumpkin, be sure to buy them whole and grind them at home in a coffee grinder of food processor before eating to unlock the essential nutrients inside.

I had never made this before and had never really been inspired to until I tried this with the stuffed peppers that Sarah made for lunch one day in school. I couldn't stop drizzling this over the ground beef. The lemon juice gives it such a delightful flavor; I would recommend just keeping the bowl of it next to your plate with spoon in hand…you'll need it.

-Tanda

ENCHILADA SAUCE

INGREDIENTS

1 medium yellow onion, chopped

2 tablespoons organic butter

½ teaspoon cardamom

½ teaspoon allspice

1 teaspoon cumin

1 tablespoon paprika

½ teaspoon sea salt

4 cloves garlic, minced

1 teaspoon sugar (optional)

1 (6 ounce) can tomato paste

2 cups chicken bone broth (see page 148)

Sauté onion in butter over medium heat until translucent and soft. Add all spices including garlic and salt and sauté 2 minutes more. Then add sugar if you like a sweeter sauce, tomato paste, and broth and let simmer over low heat until you are ready to assemble the enchiladas. If you are making the sauce ahead of time, simmer for 20 minutes to combine flavors, jar, and save.

Try This:
This recipe is amazing made with slow-roasted tomatoes (see page 109) instead of tomato paste.

Health Tip:
Ground spices such as cardamom, allspice, and cumin are aromatic spices, with their flavor being dependent on the smell more than their taste. Cardamom relieves stomach cramps and is antispasmodic. Allspice is antibacterial and antifungal, supporting the immune system. Cumin boosts the absorption of other nutrients in the foods it accompanies.

It seems to be that every cook has his or her "thing" he or she has a particular knack for. My thing is all things liquid: soups, sauces, and dressings. I find great satisfaction in making these flavorful additions from scratch, and they are much less work than one would think.

-Sarah

I have to testify to this, and I think Sarah is being modest. She is amazing at anything liquid: sauces, soups, dressings, drinks, or marinades. I stand in the kitchen with her in awe of how she just whips these up.

Let me paint the picture for you: I say, "I was wondering if you could come up with a salad of some sort tonight." She says, "What are you making?" I tell her. Then I see the wheels turning and her rummaging through cupboards and pulling out spices, and herbs, and vinegars, and oils, and a mason jar. She places it all on the counter and then just starts pouring things into this pint-sized mason jar. When satisfied, she puts the lid on, shakes, and pours over whatever greens she's thrown together in a bowl.

The salad is served, and the dinner crowd takes one bite and is fighting over the salad tongs. It's fun to watch.

-Tanda

BASIL PESTO

INGREDIENTS

2 cups loosely packed basil leaves, washed a nd dried thoroughly

2 tablespoons pine nuts, toasted

2 tablespoons parmesan, freshly grated

¼ teaspoon garlic, minced

½ teaspoon sea salt

¼ cup plus 1 tablespoon extra-virgin olive oil

Freshly ground black pepper to taste

In a food processor, combine the basil, pine nuts, parmesan, garlic, and salt, and puree. While the motor is running, drizzle in the oil until incorporated. Season with pepper to taste. Use immediately or store in the refrigerator with a piece of plastic wrap placed right on the surface of the pesto to prevent discoloration, for up to 3 days.

Try This:

This is a great way to preserve summer basil. Make a bunch and freeze it for the winter months when you're craving a bit of summer tastes.

Health Tip:

The smell of fresh basil can fill a room and take you back to the summer months of heirloom tomatoes, sweet corn, and sun. This herb can not only taste delicious in salads, on pasta, or by itself, it can also help combat stress, help with indigestion and headaches, and even help prevent cancer. Use the essential oil to help cheer the heart and the mind.

The first time I had basil pesto I was living in Colorado. I took one bite of it and was instantly in love. I couldn't understand why everything wasn't rolled and coated in this delicious greenness. Basil is one of those smells that is unmistakably summer, so take advantage of this when it's in season and warm up your food processor.

-Tanda

CILANTRO PESTO

INGREDIENTS

2 cups packed cilantro
(about one large bunch)

1 Serrano pepper
(seeded for less heat)

4 cloves garlic

¼ cup pine nuts

½ cup organic olive oil

Sea salt and freshly
ground pepper to taste

½ cup parmesan cheese
*(if you can tolerate dairy
otherwise just omit it)*

Combine cilantro, Serrano, garlic, and pine nuts and pulse in food processor until coarsely chopped. Add oil and pulse until smooth. Season with salt and pepper, then fold in cheese in medium mixing bowl. Combine pesto with additional ¼ cup olive oil and ½ cup–1 cup vinegar of your choice for a quick health salad dressing. Top grilled veggies or meats with pesto for a fresh herb-flavor punch.

Try This:

Try other fresh herbs, such as Italian parsley with sun-dried tomatoes, instead of Serrano, or Thai Basil pesto with ginger instead of garlic and a splash of lime.

Health Tip:

Cilantro chelates heavy metals such as mercury and lead from the body. Parsley has three times the vitamin C per gram than oranges do.

We made this last summer at the market and it was an overwhelming hit. People who said that they didn't like cilantro even jumped with food joy when they tasted it. We did it again at the market this past summer and had the very same reaction. This one takes people by surprise and it is just a pleasure to watch them eat it and experience cilantro in a whole new light.

-Tanda

SOUPS

There's something so satisfying about staying home on a Sunday afternoon and filling the house with sweet and savory aromas from a boiling pot of soup on the stove. With soups, the sky is the limit; you can eat them hot, cold, add fresh or dried spices and herbs, leave them chunky, or puree for a creamy experience. They are great leftovers and work really well for an on-the-go lunch.

Curling up with a steaming bowl of homemade soup, a slice of gluten-free bread loaded with fresh organic butter, and a good book is a set-up for the perfect day. Enjoy these and play around with combinations and flavors. We highly recommend having a hand blender or a food processor for easy pureeing.

-Tanda

HOMEMADE STOCKS

Homemade stock or "bone broth" is one of the most delicious immune-supporting ingredients in your kitchen. Boil bones of chicken, pheasant, beef, or wild game for twenty-four to seventy-two hours with a splash of vinegar to extract health-supporting minerals and immune-boosting compounds. Bone broth is a great home remedy for the common cold, osteoporosis, recovery from strenuous exercise, menstrual cramps, cancer, and adding health in any case of chronic disease.

-Sarah

RECIPES

BONE BROTH

Instructions

The usual way we make this is to save all the bones after roasting a whole chicken. After dinner I will debone any leftover meat and toss all the bones in a large stock pot, cover with water, add a couple of dashes of vinegar, and let simmer overnight. (The acidity of the vinegar helps extract more minerals from the bones). In the morning I will pull out some of the largest bones and crack them open on a cutting board with a wooden spoon. This exposes the marrow inside. I place the cracked bones back into the broth, add another couple of dashes of vinegar, and keep simmering all day. The longer you simmer, the more minerals you'll extract. I usually simmer chicken stock for 24 hours and lamb and beef 72 hours. (Add a splash of vinegar every 12 hours).

The last night, I will drain the broth though a colander into glass jars for later use. Keep the broth in the fridge or freezer and drink on its own with salt or use in soups, sauces, and instead of water when cooking grains.

You also can go to a local grocery store and get some beef, lamb, chicken, or turkey bones. You may have to ask your butcher if they are stored in the back. Many butchers no longer keep these, as it is rare for anyone to ask for them, so you might set up an agreement with your butcher that if he saves you a few weeks worth, you'll come take them off his hands. Often butchers won't even charge you, as they would have thrown the bones out anyway.

Options:

Skimming: You can bring broth to boil and skim the fat off the top. I usually don't do this with chicken, because this is some great stuff, but I always do it with beef. The skimmed layer also makes a great treat for your dog if you don't want to keep it in the broth.
Add any veggies, herbs, or garlic you'd like (this is not necessary, just for taste).

Try This:

Use a whole chicken or turkey including wings and neck. Cover with water and simmer with your choice of herbs, etc., until the flesh is cooked. Remove the whole bird and take the flesh from the bones. Put the bones back into the pot, add a splash of vinegar, and simmer for another 24 hours. Keep the flesh in the fridge to use for chicken soup, curry, stir-fry, or whatever you wish.

Health Tip:

Bone broth contains minerals that the body can easily recognize and absorb. It is high in calcium, magnesium, phosphorus, silicon, and sulfur. Because it's cooked for so long, the bones end up breaking down, so you also get glucosamine and chondroitin. Save money on supplements and drink bone broth. We prescribe this for patients with osteoporosis, Crohn's disease, celiac disease, ulcerative colitis, cancer, malabsorption conditions, kidney or gall stones, any immune deficiency, chronic colds and flus, and for kiddos with difficulty with growth or development.

VEGETABLE BROTH

INGREDIENTS

1 ½ quarts filtered water

2 potatoes, unpeeled

1 cup carrots,
roughly chopped

1 cup celery,
roughly chopped

1 cup of other
available vegetables
(onion, parsnips, yams,
or sweet potatoes)

¼ teaspoon cayenne

1 teaspoon oregano,
thyme, or other
desired herbs

Basil, parsley,
or cilantro to garnish

Sea salt to taste

Serves 6-8

Use stainless steel, enameled, or earthenware pot to prepare. Add all ingredients and bring to a boil, then turn down heat to a simmer. Cover and cook slowly for at least 30 minutes. Strain and serve hot.

Try This:

Add raw minced garlic and or ginger for additional health benefits and yummy flavor.

Health Tip:

This nourishing broth is used to help with body healing, reduces acidity, and increases alkalinity with potassium and sodium. To use therapeutically, drink 4-8 cups a day. This broth is especially helpful when used for:

- Post-op recovery
- Chemotherapy
- GI disturbances, i.e., gastritis, colitis, gastroenteritis, etc.
- General detoxification
- Fall or winter cleanse program

This recipe actually comes from the files of our health handouts from our Naturopathic Medical School clinic. It's hard to say how far back this dates as a great old remedy for general health and healing, but the old wisdom of soup and broths for healing the sick now has a clear scientific basis as being an effective way to add health.
-Sarah

GLUTEN-FREE CHICKEN NOODLE SOUP

INGREDIENTS

2 tablespoons
organic butter

1 medium onion, diced

4 large carrots, chopped

4 celery stalks, chopped

2 quarts bone broth
(see page 148)

½ teaspoon dried thyme,
or 1 teaspoon fresh

5 cloves garlic, minced

½ pound cooked
chicken breast, diced

½ cup parsley, chopped

Sea salt

Freshly ground
black pepper

1 (8 ounce) package
rice noodles, best
with spirals or linguini

2 tablespoons
organic olive oil

Serves 6-8

Melt butter over medium heat in a large stock/soup pot. Add onions and sauté until soft and brown. Add carrots and celery and cook 2 additional minutes. Add bone broth, thyme, and garlic, and bring to a boil. Turn down heat and simmer for 20 minutes. Add chicken and cook an additional 10 minutes. Add parsley and salt and pepper to taste at end of cooking.

While soup is cooking, boil water for rice noodles or other GF pasta. Cook pasta as directed on the package. (Do not cook pasta directly in the soup or store soup with pasta in it. Rice pasta will turn to mush when stored in liquids.)

Drain pasta and toss with 2 tablespoons olive oil.

To serve, add 1 serving of pasta to a bowl and ladle soup over it.

Try This:
Divide soup into pint-sized mason jars, leaving 1 inch of room at the top. Close with lids and freeze to pull out for a great lunch, snack, or when a family member comes down with a cold.

Health Tip:
One of my patients was diagnosed with cancer last fall, so we started working together and I told him about making broths. A month went by, and in our follow-up appointment, he said he couldn't drink enough of the stuff. His body was craving this nurturing food for a reason. When we crave foods, listen to that craving; our body doesn't make mistakes, and if we pay attention, we will hear what it's really trying to say, and what it really needs for optimal health.

Making this soup is one of our favorite weekend afternoon activities: sitting in front of the stove, wooden spoon in hand, stirring a big pot of comfort food, then curling up with a bowl of it, a slice of gluten-free bread with gobs of butter, and a good movie. And this dish, as my dad would say, "cures all that ails you."
-Tanda

CHICKEN STOCK

INGREDIENTS

Backs, necks, wings, gizzards, and the bones from a deboned chicken from the night before

Enough water to cover the bones

2 tablespoons vinegar

1 large onion, coarsely chopped

2 carrots, coarsely chopped

3 celery stalks, coarsely chopped

1 bay leaf

2 cloves

1 bunch fresh herbs like parsley, oregano, thyme, marjoram

Sea salt

Freshly ground black pepper

Place all the ingredients in a large stockpot and bring to a boil, and then reduce to a simmer for 6-12 hours. I don't skim any of the scum off the top; this is the good stuff. You may, though, if you wish.

Put it in the fridge and chill. You can scrape the fat off the top and use it for cooking or feed it to the dog. Pour everything into a large bowl through a mesh sieve and decant into a mason jar for storage.

Try This:

Play around with the different herb combinations. You can add bay leaves or a big bunch of thyme. You can also add salt to taste if you wish. The first time I made this, I had a major conundrum; what to do with the bones, meat, and veggies that were left over? Here are a few options:

Strip off all the meat from the bones, chop it up along with all the veggies, and add them back in for extra nutrients.

Chop everything up (minus the bones) and feed it to your dog or cat.

Throw them away and feel guilty about it.

Health Tip:

All broths are wonderful for colds and flus, and for promoting healthy joints, bone growth, and digestion. We tell some of our patients to drink 1–4 cups a day to add health.

Homemade stock is easy and so much better than the store-bought equivalent. We make a big batch and then decant into quart jars and stick them in the freezer. I always have one thawed in the fridge for making polenta, rice, soups, or just drinking when I feel the need. I'm also a huge proponent of not wasting food, and this is a great way to put the whole chicken to use.

-Tanda

BEEF STOCK

INGREDIENTS

4 pounds beef bones
3 pounds meaty rib
or neck bones

3 onions,
coarsely chopped

3 carrots,
coarsely chopped

3 celery stalks,
coarsely chopped

4 or more quarts water

6 sprigs of fresh thyme

2 bay leaves

1 teaspoon
peppercorns, crushed

2-12 tablespoons vinegar

1 bunch parsley

Preheat the oven to 350°F.

Place the bones in a roasting pan and brown them in the oven. When well browned, remove and add them, along with the fat, to a large stockpot along with the vegetables. Add the water, enough to cover the bones. Bring to a boil. Skim the film off the top. Then reduce heat and add the thyme, bay leaves, crushed peppercorns. Add 2 tablespoons of vinegar then add additional 2 tablespoons every 12 hours of cooking. Simmer for 12–72 hours, the longer the better, to extract as much of the minerals and nutrients as possible. Add the parsley just before finishing. Simmer another 7 minutes or so.

Remove bones with a slotted spoon. Strain the stock into a large bowl. Let it cool in the refrigerator and then remove the congealed fat that will rise to the top. Decant into mason jars and put them in the freezer for long-term storage. Fill only ¾ full, as liquid expands when it's frozen and we don't want glass all over your freezer.

Try This:
Use this for soups, meaty stews, or cooking wild rice.

Health Tip:
Broths are one of the most nourishing foods. Drink 1-4 cups when you feel a cold coming on, or you can give to kids and family with weak constitutions.

Don't be afraid of this recipe; when it is cooking, it looks (and smells) a bit "off," but push on and trust us, it's not. Adding some beef flesh in at the end greatly improves the flavor.

-Tanda

GINGER CARROT SOUP

INGREDIENTS

6 cups bone broth (see page 147)

1 large yellow onion, diced

1 stick plus 2 tablespoons organic butter

1 pound carrots, cut into 1-inch cubes

1 large yam, cut into 1-inch cubes

2-inch thumb fresh ginger, sliced

1 teaspoon sea salt

1 (16-ounce) can coconut milk

¼ cup fresh cilantro, chopped

Serves 6-8

Heat broth in large stock pot; set aside. While broth is heating, sauté onion in 2 tablespoons butter.

Add sautéed onions, carrots, yams, ginger, and salt to hot stock and bring to a boil. Turn heat down to a simmer and cook until veggies are soft, about 20 minutes. Turn off heat. Using hand blender or food processor, puree soup until smooth, about 5 minutes or more if using hand blender. (This always takes longer than I think it should to really get the carrots creamy).

Return soup to pot and stir in coconut milk and the remaining stick of butter until melted.

Garnish with fresh cilantro.

Try This:

This soup can be made with any combination of root veggies, such as parsnips, turnips, sweet potatoes, rutabagas, or yellow beets. Try adding 2 tablespoons curry powder in addition to or instead of ginger for a different flavor.

Health Tip:

Most of us know carrots are high in antioxidants and beta carotene, but what you may not know is ginger and curry powder are both potent anti-inflammatory medicines used for centuries in India for their healing properties. Curry is also full of antioxidants that can help prevent heart disease, cancer, and diabetes.

This is another invention during my time in Costa Rica. This soup was a favorite lunch during the rainy season. The volunteers would come in from building the bamboo house for the Dutchman up the road, sopping wet and tired, ready for a bowl of this soup and some homemade bread. I was still eating bread at that time, as I lived in Costa Rica before I discovered my gluten intolerance.

-Sarah

CREAMY TOMATO BISQUE WITH SLOW-ROASTED TOMATOES

INGREDIENTS

3 tablespoons organic olive oil

1 large onion, of any variety, coarsely chopped
1 large carrot, diced

1 recipe slow-roasted tomatoes, coarsely chopped (see page 108)

2 medium zucchinis, diced

2 bay leaves

4 cloves garlic, minced

1 teaspoon fresh or ½ teaspoon dried thyme

1 pint half-and-half and 1 pint bone broth, or 2 cans coconut milk, or 1 quart bone broth (see page 148)

Sea salt and freshly ground pepper

¼ cup fresh basil, cut into thin strips, for garnish

Serves 4

Heat olive oil over medium heat in a medium to large soup pot. Add onions and carrots and sauté until carrots begin to soften, about 7 minutes. Then add slow roasted tomatoes, zucchini, bay leaves, garlic and thyme. Continue cooking 2 minutes more, stirring regularly. Turn down heat to low and add liquid ingredients of your choice. Cook over low heat until veggies are soft, about 10-15 minutes. Season with salt and a few good grinds of fresh pepper to taste. Divide into bowls and garnish with fresh basil.

Try This:

If you make this with bone broth only, it can easily become a dairy-free minestrone soup. Add a 14-ounce can of cannellini beans (without liquid) to the soup when you add the tomatoes, and cook rice pasta, or other gluten-free pasta on the side. Add 1 serving of noodles to each bowl when serving. Do not add pasta to leftover soup or it will absorb all the broth overnight and leave you with a thick, casserole like dish with soggy noodles instead of soup.

Health Tip:

Adding coconut milk at the end of cooking or by only applying low heat best preserves the healthy essential fats in coconut milk by preventing oxidation. This is actually true for all fats. The less we cook them and the more we eat them in their raw state, the better they are for our health. Fats have special bonds in them that break under high heat and can actually cause the fat to go rancid more easily. Rancid, oxidized fats contribute to the inflammatory processes of heart disease, diabetes, and cancer.

Truth be told, this recipe is best made with cream, if you can tolerate dairy. If not, unsweetened coconut milk does well, or it is also delicious without any creaminess and extra broth just as a vegetable soup.
-Sarah

CHILI

INGREDIENTS

4 tablespoons butter

2 pounds ground beef

2 large onions, finely chopped

5 cloves garlic, crushed

1 tablespoon oregano

1 teaspoon cayenne

1 tablespoon ground cumin

3 tablespoons paprika

1 tablespoon sea salt

1 (28-ounce) can crushed tomatoes

1 (19-ounce) can black beans

¼ cup maple syrup or brown sugar

1 lime, juiced

1 bottle of beer

1 handful fresh cilantro, chopped

Serves 6

Melt the butter in a large pot and mix in the beef, onions, and garlic. Cook on medium-high heat until brown, stirring frequently. Add all dry seasoning and stir in for a few minutes. Add all the wet ingredients and stir in. Simmer for 2 hours partially covered. Take off heat, stir in cilantro, and serve. This dish is best served the next day after spending the night in the fridge.

Try this:

The cool thing about chili is that you can throw anything in it. Try different meats, such as ground bison, turkey, or wild game. Try using different beans, such as lentils, kidney, pinto, or even garbanzos. Even using different beers can add a whole new twist. Basically, what we've discovered is that you can't go wrong.

Health Tip:

This is a great lunch to help balance blood sugar. The protein and complex carbohydrates from the meat, beans, and veggies are going to set you up to win for the rest of the day.

There are a million and a half ways to make chili. This is courtesy of my dad, the Barefoot Gourmet, who has participated in enough chili cook-offs to perfect this recipe. It was a go-to of mine in school to make a huge batch to nibble on for the week, and with some gluten-free corn-bread, well, life doesn't get any better.

-Tanda

VEGETABLE SOUP

INGREDIENTS

2 tablespoons
organic butter

2 onions, chopped

3 garlic cloves, chopped

3 carrots, chopped

3 stalks of
celery, chopped

1 large sweet
potato, chopped

2 cups broccoli, chopped

1 (14 ounce) can
diced tomatoes

Sea salt

Freshly ground pepper

2 bay leaves

3 quarts homemade
chicken stock
(see page 148)

1 bunch parsley, chopped

Serves 6-8

Heat the butter in a large stockpot, add the onions, and sauté over low heat for about 10 minutes or until they are translucent. Add the rest of the vegetables (except the tomatoes), salt, pepper, and the bay leaves, and cook over medium heat for another 5 minutes. Add the tomatoes and stock and bring to a boil, then turn heat down to a simmer, cover, and cook for about 30 minutes or until the veggies are tender. Add the parsley, and some salt and pepper to taste. Stir and serve.

Try This:

Try other veggies, such as brussels sprouts, cabbage, kale, or parsnips. Add basil, thyme, rosemary, or cilantro instead of the parsley. You can also add beans for some fiber. This goes great with gluten-free toast with good organic butter on it.

Health Tip:

Vegetables bought locally contain more nutrients than those in the grocery store, which travel an average of 1,500 miles to sit on the shelf. To get the most out of your food, find a farmers' market in your area or go to www.localharvest.org.

This is a great way to get veggies into the family. It was a favorite of mine that my dad would make me when I came home from college and my sister and I would sit in our sunroom and eat this together. This is a great meal to freeze and bring out in the winter for some fresh summer veggies.

-Tanda

AFRICAN PEANUT SOUP

INGREDIENTS

Salsa

2 medium onions, diced

2 red or green bell
peppers, diced

½ head garlic, minced

4 large heirloom
tomatoes, diced

1 cup cilantro, minced

----

1 recipe homemade salsa
(see above or use tomato
salsa recipe on page 177)

2 tablespoons
organic olive oil

8 cups homemade
stock (see page 147)

½ teaspoon
cayenne pepper

½ teaspoon sea salt

½ teaspoon freshly
ground black pepper

½ cup uncooked
short-grain brown rice

1 (14-ounce)
can white beans

2/3 cup smooth
peanut butter

½ cup cilantro,
for garnish

Serves 6-8

Prepare salsa by combining all ingredients in a bowl. In large stock pot, sauté salsa in oil until onions begin to brown. Add stock and all seasonings and bring to a boil. Simmer 30 minutes. Add rice and beans and simmer 45-50 minutes more, until rice is cooked. Turn off heat and stir in peanut butter. Garnish with cilantro.

Try This:
Serve over half a ripe avocado in center of bowl for a complete meal.

Health Tip:
This soup is packed with protein from nonmeat sources, and the salsa adds a lot of antioxidants.

This is a great hearty, meatless soup that is nourishing to its core. Its blend of sweet and spicy makes this a great option for kids and picky adults.

-Tanda

BEEF STEW

INGREDIENTS

2 pounds chuck roast or other inexpensive cut of beef, cut into 1-inch cubes

5 tablespoons organic butter, divided

2 medium red onions, chopped

1 quart bone broth (page 147)

5 large cloves garlic, sliced

3 bay leaves

1 teaspoon fresh or ½ teaspoon dried thyme

1 teaspoon sea salt

4 large carrots, cut into ½-inch cubes

6 stalks celery, sliced

3 large potatoes, peeled and cubed

1 cup parsley, coarsely chopped

3 tablespoons gluten-free flour *(my favorite for thickening is rice flour)*

Sea salt and fresh ground pepper to taste

Serves 6

Preheat oven to 300°F.

Brown meat over high heat (if using wild game, remember to add a little oil or butter to the pan, as it has no fat in the muscle at all). Set aside. Melt 2 tablespoons butter in Dutch oven and sauté onions over medium heat until translucent. Add stew meat, broth, garlic, bay leaves, thyme, and salt to Dutch oven and bring to a simmer. Remove from heat, cover tightly in foil or a well-fitting lid, and place into preheated oven. Bake for 2 hours.

After meat is cooked to your desired tenderness, remove from oven and return to stove top over low-medium heat. Add carrots, celery, potatoes, and ¾ cup parsley to stew. Cook until veggies are tender, about 20 minutes. Turn off heat and remove 2 cups of liquid from stew. Set aside. Melt remaining 3 tablespoons butter in saucepan over low heat. Whisk in GF flour until well combined, then whisk in the 2 cups of broth. Continue to whisk, stirring constantly, until broth thickens into gravy. Add gravy to stew, garnish with remaining parsley, and serve piping hot.

Try This:
Serve with a large, crunchy green salad like the kale salad with Asian mustard dressing or a green leaf lettuce and balsamic vinaigrette (see pages 163 & 169).

Health Tip:
We often talk to our patients about the importance of food hygiene. Eating in a calm environment, in a relaxed state, and chewing your food well can make a dramatic difference in your overall health. So many of us eat in the car, in front of the television, standing up, or when we are feeling anxious or under stress. The body can't feel stress and digest food at the same time. So next time you sit down to a meal, be conscious of the emotional state you're in, chew your food thirty-one times, and turn the TV off; your body will thank you.

In our house this is venison, elk, or antelope stew. My favorite is elk for stewing, because it isn't that great for anything else but breakfast sausage. I have to tell you how funny it is for me to have an extra freezer in my garage full of meat hunted off the land here in Montana, much of which I cleaned, quartered, and butchered. I was born and raised a vegetarian for twenty-five years. Now I am pretty much a carnivore who eats meat and veggies three times a day - all for the sake of my health, and my taste buds.

-Sarah

PHÒ, VIETNAMESE BEEF NOODLE SOUP

INGREDIENTS

2 quarts beef
bone broth (see page 147)

1 thumb fresh
ginger, sliced

2 cinnamon sticks

4 pods star anise, whole

1 teaspoon fennel seed

1 teaspoon whole cloves

1 pound package
rice vermicelli

2 tablespoons olive oil

1 cup Thai basil,
whole leaves

1 cup cilantro,
slightly chopped

1 cup mint, whole leaves

1 bunch chives, chopped

1 cup bean sprouts

1 red bell pepper,
sliced into rounds

1 jalapeno, sliced

1 pound free-range,
grass-fed beef brisket,
thinly sliced

1 lime, halved, to juice
into soup when served

Serves 4

Bring broth and all dried spices to a boil; turn down heat and let simmer. Meanwhile, cook rice pasta as directed on the package. Drain, run under very cold water until cool, toss in olive oil, and set aside in a bowl in fridge. Prep all veggies and fresh herbs, arranging them on a large platter as you go. Add in raw sliced brisket to simmering broth and cook until meat is desired doneness. Turn heat off under broth.

Divide rice noodles between four bowls. Pour soup over the noodles until bowl is nearly full. I leave the whole spices in the broth and just warn others not to eat them. You can strain them out of the broth if desired. Serve bowls with platter of fresh herbs and veggies and let guests or family dress up soup as desired.

Try this:

This recipe is easily made from leftovers of the Thai steak salad (see page 82). Broth can be made ahead of time or in quantity for this to come together faster. Although there are quite a few ingredients involved in this recipe, it comes together really fast, as almost nothing needs to be chopped.

Health tip:

Eat fresh, raw herbs as much as possible

I was so bummed when I finally discovered this amazing gluten-free, dairy-free comfort food in my last year of medical school. I was bummed because I had been living next to a Phò restaurant for three years and had never tried it, so I had missed out that whole time. As we were nearing graduation and my eighty-hour-a-week schedule was getting to me, I got sick. I couldn't miss any clinics or classes, so I powered through. I ate this every day for a week, and I know it helped heal me up fast.

-Sarah

SALADS

Salads can be a great, flavorful addition to any meal, or a meal in themselves. I encourage you to think of salads as more than just a random combination of raw veggies, but as recipes where you play with texture and flavors that go well together, such as bitter and sweet, savory and salty. The dressing should complement the ingredients of the salad itself. When using more hearty or bitter ingredients, such as kale or mustard greens, a flavorful, strong dressing like the Asian mustard dressing goes well. When using fresh fruit in a salad, choose mild greens like green or red leaf lettuce, or crunchy romaine, and top with a simple oil and vinegar dressing, letting the fruit be the sweet component.

-Sarah

RECIPES

RAINBOW SALAD WITH BALSAMIC VINAIGRETTE

INGREDIENTS

For the dressing

¼ cup organic olive oil

½ cup balsamic vinegar

¼ cup real maple syrup

2 tablespoons fresh thyme

1 teaspoon sea salt

Three grinds of fresh black pepper

For the salad

1 medium beet

1 large carrot

1 large zucchini

12 large leaves of red leaf lettuce

4 ounces chevre goat cheese

Serves 4

Make the dressing by combining all ingredients in a jar with a tight fitting lid and shaking until well emulsified.

For the salad, shred the beet, carrot, and zucchini with a cheese grater or food processor, keeping each vegetable separated from the others. Divide a few large lettuce leaves between 4 small plates. Top with shredded zucchini, then carrot, then beet.

Drizzle dressing over each salad and top with 1 ounce goat cheese.

Try This:

This salad is great with pork tenderloin grilled with a citrus glaze. Also, substitute cherry tomatoes cut in half for the carrot, and cucumber for the zucchini for another delicious variation.

Health Tip:

Eating a variety of colors of fruits and vegetables is the best way to ensure you are getting all your essential vitamins and minerals. Instead of taking a multivitamin, eat a rainbow every day!

Many people don't think to shred their vegetables, but it's a fun way to change up the texture. This salad is beautiful when presented, and then, when tossed, the juice from the beets turns the whole salad a deep red.

-Tanda

MASTER DRESSING RECIPE

In my early twenties, I worked at an eco-center in Costa Rica in the middle of the jungle. Naturally, I fell into being one of the cooks feeding everyone. We made nearly everything from scratch, and that is where I put this dressing formula together.

I pretty much do the same steps every time. Start with a 1-pint glass canning jar with a tight lid. Fill the jar one third full of oil, then up to two-thirds full with vinegar, then up to a little less than full with a liquid sweetener and/or tamari. If I use dry sugar and/or salt, I add a bit more vinegar. Then top off with whatever spices or flavors you desire. Close the lid and shake until oil and vinegar are well combined. One pint will dress at least a week's worth of salads, and can be kept in the fridge up to a month.

-Sarah

Tip:
The flavors should be a little stronger than you would think in terms of salty, sweet, or spicy. A small amount of dressing will be spread over a lot of salad, and the flavors will become diluted.

Oil Ideas
Cold-pressed organic olive oil for most salads. Try using half olive and half sesame, coconut, or peanut oils for more Asian flavors.

Vinegar Ideas
Use organic raw apple cider vinegar for most salads. Other favorites are white wine vinegar, balsamic vinegar, and red wine vinegar. There are a lot of gourmet vinegars, such as champagne pomegranate and other flavors, that can be a delight to experiment with.

Sweetener Ideas
Maple syrup, brown rice syrup, agave, or raw honey. Also try using jams and preserves, such as marmalade, raspberry preserve, or orange chipotle jam.
Salty Ideas
Use 1–2 teaspoons sea salt or 1 part tamari.

Seasoning Ideas
Herbs like fresh basil, rosemary, thyme, ginger, garlic, or ground cinnamon. Fresh chili peppers, and lemon, lime, or orange juice. Add the zest of the fruit for a stronger flavor. Play around with flavored extracts like vanilla, lemon, or almond.

Creamy Ideas
Add mayo or coconut milk to give dressing a dairy-free, creamy flavor.

Health Tip:
By making your own dressings, you get to choose the finest ingredients and avoid a common source of preservatives, filler ingredients, and rancid fats. Also, making your own allows you to choose how sweet or salty you would like it, to support your blood sugar or heart health.

TRY THESE: HERE ARE THREE RECIPES TO GET YOU STARTED.

THAI GINGER VINAIGRETTE

1 part oil: ½ organic olive oil and ½ sesame oil

1 part rice wine vinegar

1 part sweet and salty: ½ honey and ½ tamari

1 teaspoon fish sauce

3-inch thumb ginger, minced

5 garlic cloves, minced

¼ cup fresh mint, chopped

¼ cup fresh cilantro, chopped

Optional: 1 hot chili, minced

Try This:

This dressing is great with Thai steak salad (see page 82) or poured over shredded cabbage as in ginger sesame slaw (see page 167).

PESTO VINAIGRETTE

1 part organic olive oil

1 part balsamic vinegar

1 part real maple syrup

1 teaspoon sea salt

½ cup fresh basil

¼ cup toasted pine nuts

¼ cup fresh grated parmesan cheese

Freshly ground black pepper
**Instead of jar, blend ingredients in blender.

Try This:

An even faster version of this is to add pre-made pesto to balsamic vinegar. Shake and serve.

BASIL LIME VINAIGRETTE

1/3 part white wine vinegar

1/3 part organic olive oil

1/3 part brown rice syrup or agave nectar

2 cups packed basil

2 cloves garlic, minced

1 teaspoon lime zest

Juice of large lime

Try This:

A lighter citrus dressing like this goes best with lighter, more delicate greens, such as a spring green mix, Boston bibb, or baby romaine. Top greens with shredded carrots and sliced red onion for color.

CUCUMBER AND TOMATO SALAD WITH RED WINE VINAIGRETTE

INGREDIENTS

For the salad

2 medium cucumbers, sliced

8 ounces cherry tomatoes, halved

2 large heirloom tomatoes, cut into ½-inch pieces

1 (10 ounce) jar kalamata olives, pitted

For the dressing

½ cup red wine vinegar

¼ cup organic olive oil

¼ cup fresh dill, chopped

1 tablespoon sugar

1 teaspoon sea salt

Serves 4-6

Combine all salad and dressing ingredients and marinate in the fridge 30 minutes before serving.

Try This:

If you have a bountiful garden, prepare this by leaving out the oil and dicing all ingredients, then putting in a jar and preserving for a delightful winter treat.

Health Tip:

Cucumbers are one of those foods whose health benefits you don't hear much about, but they are packed with benefits. They have lots of fiber and water and are soothing to the digestive system. When purchasing, look for ones that are firm with round edges and bright to dark green colors.

Justin and I were throwing a summer barbecue at our house in Portland, Oregon. I had asked Sarah to bring a salad, and this is what she came with. It was gone before any of the other food. It's so fresh, flavorful, and fun to look at, I'd suggest it become a regular for summertime meals and parties where you have to bring a dish to pass.

-Tanda

GINGER SESAME SLAW

INGREDIENTS

For the slaw
½ head of cabbage, shredded (all 1 type or a combination of red, green, bok choy, or Savoy)

2 large carrots, grated

1 bunch chives, chopped

1 cup cilantro, chopped

For the dressing
2-inch thumb of ginger, grated

½ cup rice wine vinegar

¼ cup tamari

¼ cup honey

2 tablespoons sesame oil

2 tablespoons organic olive oil

¼ cup toasted black sesame seeds

Serves 4

Combine veggies in medium salad bowl. Combine dressing ingredients in pint jar, close tightly with a lid, and shake until well emulsified. Dress, toss, and serve.

Try This:

This Asian inspired salad goes great with seared ahi tuna and a sweet fruit chutney, such as mango radish salsa (see page 179).

Health Tip:
Cabbage belongs to Brassicaceae family and is a green leafy plant like other vegetables of the same family as broccoli, cauliflower, and kale. Cabbage contains phytonutrients that protect the body from free radicals and increase the production of enzymes involved in detoxification.

You can do most anything with slaws: use them to top tacos, as a side with burgers, or a base with stir-fried meat. This has an Asian twist with a ginger bite. Add this to leftover shredded chicken, top with slivered almonds, and wrap in lettuce for an easy lunch.

-Sarah

GREEN SALAD WITH CREAMY ORANGE DRESSING

INGREDIENTS

For the dressing

½ cup apple
cider vinegar

½ cup canned coconut
milk, full fat

¼ cup real maple syrup

Juice of 1 orange

Zest of orange, julienned

½ teaspoon
vanilla extract

½ teaspoon freshly
ground nutmeg

½ teaspoon sea salt

For the salad

Large salad bowl full of
mixed greens, the more
bitter, the better
(try curly endive, kale,
dandelion greens,
mustard greens, turnip
greens or arugula)

1 orange, peeled and
thinly sliced

Serves 6

Make dressing by combining all ingredients in glass jar and shaking to combine. If coconut milk won't combine well, submerge closed jar in warm water for 5 minutes, then shake. (Coconut oil is a solid below 75 degrees).

Thoroughly toss greens and oranges in dressing and serve immediately.

Try This:

Try keeping it simple; a bowl of fresh picked greens, your favorite oil and vinegar, and a fresh herb of choice: tarragon, parsley, lemon zest, rosemary, or cilantro. Toss and serve.

Health Tip:

Coconut milk, cream, or oil—nature's best brain food. Full of mood-stabilizing, anti-depression, concentration and memory boosting saturated fats, coconut is a true superfood. Key supporters in the use of omega-3s, saturated fats are the preferred fuel for your heart. They can protect you from stroke and, when combined with a high-protein, low-carb diet, can reduce cholesterol levels, promote weight loss, and normalize insulin.

Mixing the sweet dressing and the bitter greens makes this salad unique and super tasty. Grill some chicken and slice it on top for a satisfying summer meal.

-Tanda

KALE SALAD WITH ASIAN HONEY MUSTARD DRESSING

INGREDIENTS

For the salad

1 bunch chard, chopped into ¼-inch thin strips

1 bunch kale, chopped into ¼-inch thin strips

For the dressing

¼ cup organic olive oil

¼ cup sesame oil

½ cup apple cider vinegar

¼ cup tamari

¼ cup honey

½ cup Dijon mustard

¼ cup sesame seeds

¼ cup mustard seeds

Serves 6

Add greens to a large salad bowl. Add all dressing ingredients except seeds to a pint jar (with lid).

Heat dry skillet to medium-high heat and add seeds. Occasionally toss seeds to avoid burning until seeds begin to pop off pan like popcorn.

Lastly, add seeds to jar (they will sizzle when they hit the oil—my favorite part!). Close jar with a tight lid and shake until oil and vinegar are emulsified. Dress salad thoroughly before serving.

If you prefer the greens less raw dress salad 30-60 min before serving to allow the vinegar to wilt the kale.

Try This:

Use dandelion greens, mustard greens, broccoli rabe, radicchio, or other hearty, bitter greens in this salad. Also consider adding shredded carrot or shredded raw beets.

Health Tip:

Dark, leafy, bitter greens are high in chlorophyll, a potent heavy-metal chelator, and their bitter flavor is a digestive stimulant and tonic. Mustard greens are a very warming herb for the lungs and can help defend against a chest cold or flu.

Another crowd favorite, this one takes everyone by surprise and leaves people pleading for seconds. Raw kale may seem like a tough sell, but in this recipe, even the most suspicious bystanders become raving fans.

-Sarah

WILTED GREEN SALAD

INGREDIENTS

2–3 tablespoons organic olive oil

3–4 shallots, thinly sliced

4 cloves of garlic, chopped

2–3 tablespoons of balsamic vinegar

2 bunches chard, kale, or spinach

Sea salt and freshly ground pepper

Serves 4-6

In a large skillet over medium-high heat, add the olive oil, shallots, and garlic, and cook for about a minute. Add the vinegar and cook for another 1–2 minutes, then add the greens, stirring occasionally, and cook until wilted. Season with salt and pepper. Serve warm.

Try This:

Try adding raisins or bacon, or sprinkle with goat cheese. Experiment with other vinegars, such as apple cider, red wine, or white wine vinegar. This one is also great cooked in leftover honey mustard dressing (see page 169).

Health Tip:

The dark, leafy greens are packed with calcium and vitamins B, C, K, and A. They are rich in antioxidants, are anti-inflammatory, and have cancer-fighting properties.

This is one of the first recipes we tried at the farmers' market last summer. When most people hear "kale" or "chard," they wrinkle their noses in disgust. Sarah and I would simply smile and place the small plastic cup in their hand and dish this salad into it. I'd pass them a fork, Sarah would get them a napkin, and we'd sit back and watch. One bite, and first there would be a look of confusion, and then a look of pure satisfaction, and then a big smile. Works every time.

-Tanda

TARRAGON SALAD WITH SIMPLE WHITE WINE VINAIGRETTE

INGREDIENTS

For the salad

1 head red leaf lettuce, washed and hand shredded

4 handfuls of fresh tarragon, roughly chopped

4 kiwis, pealed and roughly chopped

5 big shallots, thinly sliced

For the dressing

1/3 cup white wine vinegar

2/3 cup organic olive oil

1 teaspoon sea salt

Several good grinds of fresh black pepper

Serves 6-8

In a large salad bowl, combine all the salad fixings. Mix the dressing in a "glass jar with a lid, shake, and pour over the salad. Toss and serve.

Try This:

Try other fruits, such as red or green grapes. If you can tolerate dairy, you can shave some good parmesan over top. You can also use red wine vinegar instead of white. This goes really well with white meats, such as fish, chicken, or pork.

Health Tip:

Tarragon is a great digestive aid. It promotes production of bile and helps the liver to detoxify. It also contains high amounts of minerals, such as calcium, manganese, iron, and copper.

This salad was inspired by Jamie Oliver's book *Jamie's Kitchen*, which everyone should own. The dressing is super easy and the tarragon gives a surprise flavor that knocks everyone off his or her feet.

-Tanda

SPINACH AND STRAWBERRY SALAD WITH LEMON POPPY SEED DRESSING

INGREDIENTS

For the dressing

½ cup apple cider vinegar

½ cup organic olive oil

¼ cup real maple syrup

Zest of ½ of a lemon

Juice of whole lemon

1 teaspoon vanilla extract

¼ cup poppy seeds

½ teaspoon sea salt

For the sald

1 large bunch spinach

½ pint strawberries, washed and sliced

½ cup sliced almonds

1 small red onion, sliced thinly

Optional:

3 ounces plain chevre goat cheese, crumbled

Serves 6

In a pint jar, combine all dressing ingredients, close tightly with a lid, and shake until oil and vinegar are well emulsified. Then combine all salad ingredients except chevre in large salad bowl. Generously dress salad and toss. Add optional chevre to top.

Try This:

Because this is a sweeter salad, serve it with bitter, sour, or savory flavors such as herb roasted chicken (page 72), steak with olive tapenade, or rack of pork (see page 96).

Health Tip:

Spinach is full of essential nutrients, such as vitamins K, A, and C, manganese, foliate, magnesium, and iron. Spinach helps promote healthy bones and immunity and prevent heart disease. It increases brain function, eyesight, GI health, and energy. Get the picture? Eat your greens!

Lemon poppy seed cake is a favorite of Sarah's and mine. When we went gluten free, this was Sarah's effort to re-create the flavor of it without the gluten. It took her a few tries, and then when it dawned on her to add the vanilla extract, our whole world changed. This is a great salad for kids, too. You could even have it for dessert…it's that good.

-Tanda

APPETIZERS AND SNACKS

Appetizers are an easy way to stave off a starving family with something healthy while they wait for dinner to be done. They are also a great start to a dinner party to allow guests to mingle, have a glass of wine, get acquainted, and to allow the buzz of your party to begin. One of our favorite things is to stand in the kitchen, putting the finishing touches on the main course, and listen to our guests laugh, exchange stories, and connect. Most of these recipes can be cooked or prepped quickly and easily, and many can be made ahead of time or in quantity to have around as snacks.

These recipes can also be used as side dishes to a main meat dish for a less formal meal.

We also included a list of our favorite gluten-free, dairy-free snacks to help with the in-between mealtime. Most grocery stores now have a "gluten-free" section with lots of snack options. Also look in the bulk aisle and, of course, a whole foods base is best. So shop the periphery for fruits, veggies, jerky, nuts, and seeds. We also suggest having a food dehydrator, or at least access to one, to make your own veggie chips, dried fruit, and dried meats. If not, no worries, just use your oven.

-Tanda

RECIPES

HOW TO PLAY WITH SALSAS

There is a basic formula to making a fresh mouthwatering salsa, and once you know it you can play around with endless combinations that pop in your mouth and please the pickiest of eaters.

The salsa formula

Something from the onion family (scallions, leeks, red onion, sweet white

onion, or red onion)

Juice from the citrus family (limes, lemons, oranges, or grapefruit)

Pepper, spicy or not (basic green bell pepper all the way to habañero)

The base flavor, veggie or fruit (tomatoes, pineapple, avocado, cucumber, mango, strawberries—this is your chance to get creative!!)

An herb (cilantro, mint, basil, tarragon, try even sage or some of the other savory types)

· Don't forget the sea salt

Here are a few to get you started...

CLASSIC GARDEN TOMATO SALSA

INGREDIENTS

3 garden carrots

1 jalapeño

1 red onion

5 fresh ripe tomatoes, chopped

Juice of 1 lime

1 bunch cilantro chopped

1 tablespoon sea salt

Serves 6-8

In a food processor, place the carrots, the jalapeno, and the onion, and pulse the food processor until they are roughly chopped. Place in a large bowl. Hand chop all the tomatoes and add them to the bowl, squeeze the lime over the top, then add the chopped cilantro and the sea salt. Stir and serve with corn chips.

Try This:

Try this as an appetizer or load it on top of grilled burgers or lettuce wraps (recipe page 190).

Health Tip:

You can't go wrong with this. Everything in here adds so much health to your body. I loved sitting on the counter in the camp kitchen, watching my dad make this. After all the ingredients were in the bowl, tossed to perfection, he would tip the bowl slightly and, with a metal spoon, scoop out the juices from the bottom, put them in a cup, and drink it. He then would turn to me, smacking his lips, and say, "That stuff is God's nectar."

This is a favorite appetizer when we are sitting on the dock at our friend's summer camp in the Adirondacks. Dad makes a huge loaf of homemade bread with a giant bowl of fresh salsa, and we all stand around the table, watching the sun go down over the lake, delighting in this sweet, fresh slice of heaven.

-Tanda

SOUTHWESTERN SALSA

INGREDIENTS

2 garden carrots

1 jalapeño

1 red onion

3 fresh ripe tomatoes

3 ears of corn with kernels removed

1 (14 ounce) can of drained black beans

Juice of 1 lime

1 bunch cilantro, chopped

1 tablespoon sea salt

Serves 6-8

In a food processor, place the carrots, the jalapeño, and the onion, and pulse the food processor until they are roughly chopped. Place in a large bowl. Hand chop all the tomatoes and add them to the bowl, along with the corn and black beans, squeeze the lime over the top, then add the chopped cilantro and the sea salt. Stir and serve with corn chips.

Try This:

Pair this appetizer with steak tacos as a colorful side dish (see page 81). You could even try excluding the beans to make a fabulous corn salsa.

Health Tip:

The combination of corn and beans provides both carbohydrate and protein. Beans are also loaded with fiber, which provides support to the digestive track.

This is a classic to go over huevos rancheros (see page 62) and is a fun twist to the everyday tomato salsa.
-Tanda

MANGO RADISH SALSA

INGREDIENTS

2 ripe mangos, peeled
and cut into small chunks

1 red onion,
finely chopped

6 red radishes, chopped

2 scallions, chopped

Juice of ½ a lime

1 large handful of fresh
cilantro, chopped

1 jalapeño pepper,
chopped (remove seeds
if you want less heat)

Sea salt to taste

Serves 6-8

Put all ingredients in a bowl, toss, and serve.

Try This:

Serve with corn chips for a quick, easy appetizer or over fish (tuna, halibut, trout, or salmon).

Health Tip:

Radishes are a great source of dietary fiber; they are also high in vitamins like C, K, and B6. They contain essential minerals, such as potassium, calcium, magnesium, copper, and manganese. And because of their known antibacterial and antifungal properties, they have been found to be effective in helping cure lung infections and digestive aliments.

I made this up last summer when Sarah and I were at the farmers' market. I had called the farmers to see what was coming out of the ground that week, and all of them said radishes. "Hmm," I thought, "well, salsa sounds good." So this is what I came up with, and it was a huge hit with the locals of Bozeman. I'm sure it will be for you, too.

-Tanda

PINEAPPLE CUCUMBER SALSA

INGREDIENTS

3 fully ripe jalapeños
(or less, depending
on desired heat)

1 large red or white onion

3 scallions, chopped

2 teaspoons sea salt

Juice of 1 lime

1 pineapple, coarsely
hand chopped

2 fresh cucumbers,
chopped

1 handful of fresh
cilantro, chopped

Serves 6-8

In a food processor, finely chop the peppers. Add cut-up onions, salt, and lime juice, and coarsely chop together. Put in a mixing bowl. Stir in the pineapple, cucumbers, and cilantro. Let rest an hour before stirring again and serving. Will last up to 2 weeks sealed in the fridge.

Try This:

Serve with corn chips as a show-stopping appetizer. Put over grilled tuna steaks, or it makes a great side next to grilled chicken.

Health Tip:

All of the hot peppers are wonderful for cardiovascular health. They help with circulation issues and those people with a cold constitution. Cucumbers are primarily composed of water, but also contain high levels of vitamin C. Pineapple contains bromelain, which is a natural anti-inflammatory and helps with digestion.

Justin worked for a delivery company the first few months that we lived in Portland, Oregon. He would wake at the crack of dawn and drive off to deliver fresh goods to the local stores. He would come home with whatever leftovers they had. One night he came home with his arms full of these salsas and a giant grin on his face. "T, you gotta try this." He cracked one of them open and we dipped in. It was a delicious, flavorful combo of pineapple, cucumber, and orange juice. We sat there and ate it until it was gone. Since then, I have made my own version, and it's one of the freshest-tasting salsas out there.

-Tanda

BEET PUREE

INGREDIENTS

1 pound beets, chopped into 1-inch cubes

2–3 tablespoons organic apple cider vinegar

Salt to taste

Sprig of parsley to garnish

Serves 6-8

Boil beets in water until you can easily put a fork through them (about 20 minutes). Drain beets and add vinegar. Puree in the pot with a hand blender or blend in a food processor until smooth. Add salt to taste, transfer to serving bowl, and add parsley to garnish.

Try This:
Make your own veggie dips with different root veggie purees, such as beets, carrots, parsnips, sunchokes, celeriac, yams, sweet potatoes, or even winter squash. Serve with rice or other gluten-free crackers.

Health Tip:
Beets are one of the champions out there for their high levels of antioxidants and cancer-fighting properties. You really can't eat enough of them…although they do have a laxative effect, so beware.

We put on a big dinner a while back for some of the students at Montana State University. We were rolling around ideas for what to make for dinner. We had decided on pork ribs, creamy polenta, and a summer salad, but what to do for an appetizer that would open their eyes to new ways of eating? Sarah came up with this one and it was a huge hit. We did three different purees and had them guess what veggie they were eating, along with what the hidden ingredient was. Kind of a fun game to play with your guests, and keeps them involved with their food, chewing, tasting, and experiencing what's going on in their mouth.

-Tanda

CARROT GINGER PUREE

INGREDIENTS

1 pound carrots, chopped
into 1-inch sections

2-inch thumb of fresh
ginger, chopped

2 tablespoons
organic butter

Sea salt to taste

Sprig of parsley to garnish

Serves 6-8

Boil carrots in water until you can easily put a fork through them (about 20 minutes). Drain carrots and add chopped ginger and butter. Puree all ingredients in the pot with a hand blender or in a processor until smooth. Add salt to taste, transfer to serving bowl, and add parsley to garnish.

Try This:

Explore the root veggies you don't usually use to make new combos, such as Jerusalem artichokes (also called sunchokes) with lemon juice and butter, and celeriac (or celery root) with butter and parsley blended in.

Health Tip:

Starchy root veggies are a great, satisfying alternative to bread, rice, or other high-carbohydrate foods in a meal. Eating bread, pasta, and rice spikes the blood sugar and thus insulin, stressing out the adrenal glands and potentially causing damage to the artery walls.

Ginger and carrot were made for each other, and ginger is so great for digestion and heart health. Add it whenever you can, by the spoon or even fist full.

-Tanda

HEIRLOOM BRUSCHETTA

INGREDIENTS

5 tablespoons
organic olive oil divided

3 tablespoons
balsamic vinegar divided

3 cloves garlic,
finely chopped

1 bunch basil, split in
half and chopped

Sea salt

Freshly ground pepper

1 loaf gluten-free bread,
with each slice cut in half

4–5 heirloom tomatoes,
chopped

1 red onion,
finely chopped

4 scallions, chopped

Serves 6-8

Preheat oven to 425°F.

In a small bowl mix 4 tablespoons olive oil, 2 tablespoons balsamic, garlic, half of the basil, salt, and pepper; set aside. On a cookie sheet, lay out the pieces of bread and spread on the olive oil and balsamic mixture. Place in the oven for 5–7 minutes until the bread is toasted and crispy. Remove from oven and set aside.

In a large mixing bowl, add the tomatoes, onion, scallions, the other half of the basil, 1 tablespoon olive oil, 1 tablespoon balsamic, salt, and pepper.

Place about 1 tablespoon of the tomato mixture on each of the slices of toast. Put back in the oven for another 3–5 minutes. Remove, plate, and serve.

Try This:
Use different herbs like mint, cilantro, dill, and parsley. You can even use parsley in the olive oil base and then basil in the tomato mixture for different flavors. Try topping the tomatoes with goat cheese and let that melt in the oven. This is a great crowd pleaser served before a summer meal of grilled chicken and corn on the cob.

Health Tip:
Tomatoes are a rich source of cancer-fighting nutrients. They also contain high levels of vitamin C and A and are packed with antioxidants.

If you can get Heirloom tomatoes purchase them whenever you can. The flavors, textures, and colors are worth every cent. You can use regular tomatoes, but the heirlooms take this to a new level. This recipe is a lot of fun playing around with all the different tasty combinations of flavors, and makes for a great appetizer.

-Tanda

CAPRESE SALAD

INGREDIENTS

2 large farm-fresh tomatoes

3 balls of buffalo mozzarella, or goat cheese if dairy intolerant

1 bunch fresh basil

Organic olive oil

Balsamic vinegar

Sea salt

Freshly ground black pepper

Serves 4-6

Slice the tomatoes in ¼-inch-thick slices, place on a serving plate, and sprinkle liberally with the sea salt and freshly ground pepper. Slice the mozzarella in ¼-inch slices and place 1 over each tomato. Place 1 leaf of basil over the top of the mozzarella. Drizzle the olive oil and balsamic over each of the tomato/ mozzarella stacks. Liberally salt and pepper to taste and serve.

Try This:

Try using different varieties of tomatoes, such as heirloom, yellow, and green tomatoes, to play with color variations. This is a great summer dish and a terrific salad to bring to your next barbecue.

Health Tip:

Tomatoes are rich in lycopene and other antioxidants. Basil has antioxidant, antibacterial, and anti-inflammatory properties. Mozzarella contains calcium and protein.

This is a summer classic that will make your taste buds smile. Basil straight from the garden is clean, fresh, and the epitome of summer. So when the tomatoes and the basil ripen in July, eat this and savor every bite.

-Tanda

SMOKED SALMON CUCUMBERS

INGREDIENTS

2–3 tablespoons

1 English cucumber, sliced

1 pound package smoked wild caught salmon

Crème fraiche or a soft goat cheese

2 shallots, thinly sliced

Capers

Dill, chopped

Course sea salt

Freshly ground pepper (white, green or black)

Serves 6-8

Stack the above ingredients in the order listed, sprinkle with salt and pepper, and serve chilled.

Try This:

Use fresh veggies such as sliced cucumber, sliced tomatoes, sliced carrots, cabbage leaves, romaine lettuce leaves, or jicama as the base of appetizers instead of crackers or bread.

Health Tip:

Salmon is a cold-water, deep-sea fish rich in protein and healthy fats, including omega-3s. Also, crème fraiche is a source of immune-healthy fats and fat-soluble vitamins, such as vitamins A, D, E, and K. Always use whole-fat dairy products, as they are less processed and contain more of these essential nutrients.

Smoked salmon is such a treat, and for someone who's not a huge fan of fish, I love this dish. When we lived in Portland, Oregon, we had some of the most amazing smoked salmon that made this dish one of my favorites to serve when hosting dinner parties. It's really easy, quick, and there's no cooking involved, which frees up the stove and oven for your main course.

-Tanda

STEAMED ARTICHOKES WITH LEMON CAPER BUTTER

INGREDIENTS

4 fresh artichokes

½ stick of organic butter

1 tablespoon capers

Juice of ½ a lemon

1–2 tablespoons fresh chopped parsley

½ teaspoon sea salt

Freshly ground pepper

Serves 6-8

4 fresh artichokes ½ stick of organic butter 1 tablespoon capers Juice of ½ a lemon 1–2 tablespoons fresh chopped parsley ½ teaspoon sea salt Freshly ground pepper

Place the artichokes in a steamer basket (or a pot of water) with at least 3 cups water and steam, covered, until the leaves can be pulled out easily, about 1 hour. Remove from pot and let cool. About halfway through cooking, check to see if you need to add more water.

In a small bowl, place the remaining ingredients, then microwave or heat in a small saucepan until butter is melted. Stir and serve with artichokes.

Try This:

Make extra and reheat in the microwave for a tasty, healthy afternoon snack or addition to lunch.

Health Tip:

Artichokes are very healing and detoxifying to the liver. The liver is the largest internal organ and is responsible for a wide range of functions, one of them being detoxification. When the liver is overstressed, the whole body is affected, and symptoms may appear, such as headaches, muscle pain, fatigue, skin irritation, and emotional imbalances.

People often ask me how to cook these things, and I promise they're not as intimidating as they may look—and there's nothing like a fresh artichoke. The Portland Farmers' Market was the first time I'd ever had one, and it blew me away. They were meaty and sweet and turned a beautiful, brilliant green when I boiled them. Anytime you can get your hands on one that has just been picked, I highly recommend it.

This recipe is a great appetizer, and when I cook for my friends, this is one dish that is often requested.

-Tanda

GUACAMOLE

INGREDIENTS

2 small tomatoes, chopped

Juice of 1 lime

1 clove garlic, minced

1 teaspoon sea salt

1 jalapeño, chopped and seeds removed

5 ripe avocados

1 handful fresh cilantro, chopped

Serves 6

In a bowl put the tomatoes, lime juice, garlic, salt, and jalapeño. Scoop the avocados into the bowl and, with a knife, cut them into small chunks and stir into the other ingredients. Add cilantro, stir, and serve with freshly baked GF baguettes or chips.

Try This:
It's a great topping for burgers or white fish, grilled ahi tuna, or in lettuce wraps.

Health Tip:
Avocados are a rich source of vitamin K and potassium. They contain anti-inflammatory properties, and the fat source is one of the best you can get.

My sister-in-law claimed that she wasn't a fan of guacamole, so I made this for her one day, and now, every time I'm back East, it's a must have. It takes about three minutes and tastes like you slaved all day.
-Tanda

EASY LETTUCE WRAPS

INGREDIENTS

4 romaine leaves, whole

4 tablespoons hummus

¼ pound deli meat
(turkey, ham, roast beef,
or chicken)

¼ cup sprouts

¼ cup carrots, shredded

¼ cup cabbage, shredded

Serves 1

Lay out the lettuce leaves and fill each one with 1 tablespoon of humus, 2 slices of deli meat, and top with sprouts, carrots, and cabbage. Roll them up and enjoy!

Try This:
Experiment with an assortment of veggies and sauces; you can use mustard, pesto, roasted red peppers, salad dressings, or salsa.

Health Tip:
This is a great snack to help balance blood sugar and a great way to get those veggies in.

When Sarah and I first went gluten free during medical school, this was a great, quick, and easy lunch or snack to take with us to class or the clinic, in place of the typical sandwich. Now, in our office, we always keep these fixings in the kitchen in case we need something to munch on.

-Tanda

ROASTED RED PEPPER SAUCE

INGREDIENTS

2 red bell peppers, roasted (procedure follows) and chopped

2 tablespoons organic olive oil

3 cloves garlic

3 tablespoons fresh chives, basil, or parsley, chopped

1 tablespoon balsamic vinegar

Sea salt and pepper to taste

Serves 6-8

Roasting peppers: Lightly coat peppers in olive oil and, with a cooking fork, roast them over a gas or electric burner until the skin is blackened. Place them on a plate and cover with a metal bowl. Allow them to cool, then peel them, starting from the bottom up, removing seeds.

Place all ingredients in a food processor; blend until smooth. Serve alone with rice crackers or pour over goat cheese and dig in.

Try This:

Try adding 1 tablespoon freshly squeezed lemon juice or dash of cayenne for a spicy bite. Serve with crackers, over gluten-free pasta, over grilled veggies, or pour over goat cheese as an appetizer.

Health Tip:

The bright red, yellow, and green coloring of these vegetables lets you know that they are high in antioxidants, helping prevent and fight cancer. They are heart healthy with their high levels of vitamin B6 and folic acid. Men, eat them for prostate health, as they contain high levels of lycopene.

This was another first, this time with Trader Joe's food market. They have this fabulous roasted red pepper sauce and Sarah had it at her annual Christmas party. She had poured it over a block of local goat cheese and served it with rice crackers. There was a lot of other food there...but I don't remember it. This is our own version; pour it over goat cheese or not, it's delicious either way.

-Tanda

BLACK BEAN DIP

INGREDIENTS

2 (14 ounce) cans
black beans

4 scallions

1 plum tomato

1 bunch cilantro

1 jalapeño
(remove seeds if less
heat is desired)

1 tablespoon cumin

Sea salt to taste

Serves 6-8

Place all ingredients in a food processor and blend until smooth. Serve with corn chips, rice crackers, or gluten-free bread.

Try This:

Use different beans, such as chickpeas, white beans, even lentils. Play around with other spices to add, such as cayenne, paprika, or coriander. With the chickpeas, you can add tahini (see recipe on page 140) and lemon juice for a hummus, and for the white beans you can add tomatoes and parsley for a summery dip.

Health Tip:

Beans are a fabulous source of fiber that is important for maintaining gastrointestinal health.

Believe it or not, Trader Joe's food market was the source of the first really good black bean dip that I had a few years ago. Here's my own version. This is a great appetizer or snack. You can also use this to smear on gluten-free toast and top with a couple of fried eggs and cilantro.

-Tanda

BACON-WRAPPED ASPARAGUS

INGREDIENTS

1½ pounds of fresh spring asparagus spears

Organic olive oil

Freshly ground black pepper

4 slices of bacon

Serves 6-8

These are best grilled, but if you're using the oven, preheat to 400°F.

Coat the asparagus spears with the olive oil and season with the black pepper. Divide the number of asparagus by 4, gather them into bundles, and wrap each bundle with one of the 4 slices of bacon. If grilling, place the bundles on a hot grill, cover, and cook about 10–15 minutes until bacon is crispy. If using the oven, place the bundles on a cookie sheet or slotted broiler pan and bake about 12 minutes.

Try This:

You can use pancetta instead of the bacon. You can also try sprinkling with herbs, such as rosemary, sage, thyme, or chives.

Health Tip:

Asparagus is very high in foliate, which is essential for a healthy cardiovascular system. The nutrients in the asparagus spears also help detoxify the liver and help the kidneys rid the body of waste material.

We served this at the farmers' market last summer with bacon from Amaltheia Organic Dairy here in Belgrade, Montana, and we couldn't keep it on the table. People were licking their fingers and coming back for rounds two and three. Your guests and family will do the same.

-Tanda

SAUTÉED MUSHROOMS WITH GARLIC AND THYME

INGREDIENTS

2 pounds mixed mushrooms, such as crimini, shitake, porcini, morels, and portobellos

½ cup organic olive oil

3 shallots, chopped

4 tablespoons organic butter

4 cloves garlic, chopped

1 handful fresh thyme, chopped

Sea salt and freshly ground pepper to taste

Serves 6-8

Clean mushrooms with a towel or sponge, then slice them thickly.

Heat the olive oil in a large saucepan or Dutch oven. Add the shallots and cook over low heat until they are translucent, about 5 minutes. Add the butter, garlic, mushrooms, thyme, salt, and pepper, and cook over medium heat until the mushrooms are tender, about 8–10 minutes, stirring them often.

Try This:

Serve them over a grilled steak or hamburger. You can add other herbs, too, such as parsley, rosemary, or sage. After you serve, you could sprinkle with goat cheese.

Health Tip:

Thyme is antibacterial and a wonderful antioxidant. It's been used for centuries to treat chest and respiratory problems, such as coughs and congestions.

The first time I remember having really great sautéed mushrooms was in Sun Valley, Idaho, when I was a live-in nanny. Abby, the mother of the two boys, would have me chop the mushroom while she melted a lot of butter in a frying pan. While the butter was just beginning to foam, she turned to me and said, "The key to mushrooms is butter." And when we sat down at the table that night and I took my first bite, I could only agree with her.

-Tanda

BROILED PORTOBELLOS

INGREDIENTS

4–6 portobello
mushrooms

Sea salt

Freshly ground
black pepper

1 cup organic
butter, melted

1 handful parsley

Serves 6-8

Preheat oven to 400°F.

Remove stems from the mushrooms and place them cup side up on a baking
sheet. Sprinkle liberally with sea salt and pepper, and then drizzle the butter over them. Place them in the oven for 6-7 minutes. Remove; cut them into
wedges, sprinkle with finely chopped parsley (optional), and serve.

Try This:
Sprinkle different fresh herbs on top before cooking, such as rosemary, thyme,
or sage.

Health Tip:
Portobello and crimini mushrooms are very high in selenium, a potent antioxidant and an essential nutrient for healthy thyroid function.

Portobellos are one of my favorite mushrooms; they are meaty and rich
and don't need a lot of fussing with to taste amazing. This is a super
simple, satisfying appetizer that I serve on a big white plate. Garnish
with finely chopped parsley and serve with toothpicks or wooden skew-
ers and let the guests dig in.

-Tanda

COCONUT BERRY BLISS

INGREDIENTS

4 cups mixed
berries (blueberries,
strawberries, blackberries,
cherries, raspberries,
or huckleberries)

2 cups coconut milk

1 sprig of mint, to garnish

Serves 4

Divide the berries up into 4 bowls and pour about ½ cup of coconut milk over each serving. Serve as dessert, breakfast, or just a perfect summer snack.

Try This:

Try some freshly chopped mint over the top, or cinnamon or nutmeg.

Health Tip:

Berries are potent little packages offering rich antioxidants due to their color. The substances that make a blueberry blue are anthocyanins, credited with being protective against cancer, the aging process, heart disease, infection, inflammation, and more. Berries are also rich in quercetin, a bioflavonoid, which is anti-allergy.

The sheer beauty of this dish is enough to want to dive into it daily. We hosted a dinner party where we served this at the end of a mid summer meal of fire roasted leg of lamb, grilled eggplant with basil and a green salad. Our guests crowded around me as I dished up the red, white, and blue into martini glasses, with their eyes feasting and mouths watering, and then one of them declared, spoon in hand, "I cant eat this! It's too pretty!" and then I watched as she scooped a mouth full and grinned with a sweet satisfaction.

-Tanda

ABOUT THE AUTHORS

Sarah Marshall, ND, graduated from the University of Utah in Salt Lake City, Utah, with a degree in chemistry and then received a doctorate of naturopathic medicine from the National College of Natural Medicine in Portland, Oregon.

A visionary in the advancement of holistic medicine Dr. Marshall practices as a naturopathic physician and holistic health coach in her international telemedicine practice. Her primary focus is to empower her clients to overcome illness, fatigue, and weight problems to live full and satisfying lives that naturally generate and maintain health.

Dr. Marshall artfully bridges the gap between the hearts desire, mental-emotional imbalance and the resulting state of health of the physical body truly practicing holistic medicine at is core. Focusing on food as medicine, strength and flexibility of body, hormone balance, and mental-emotional peace she treats a range of diseases and disorders including but not limited to allergies, infertility, hormonal issues, cardiovascular disease, weight challenges, diabetes, autoimmune disease and cancer.

Dr. Marshall is an international educator and speaker of the holistic healthcare model. She currently resides in Scottsdale, Arizona, and, when not practicing medicine, can be found traveling the world, skiing, hiking, running, sailing, and generally having the dream adventures of a lifetime.

Tanda Cook, ND, graduated from Skidmore College in Saratoga Springs, New York, with a degree in biology and then continued on to receive a doctorate of naturopathic medicine from the National College of Natural Medicine in Portland, Oregon.

Dr. Cook is an expert in restoring the innate congruence between mental emotional phenomena and the physical body resulting in exception high levels of health. Combining a symphonic blend of destination medicine and long term health consulting. Dr. Cook practices as a naturopathic physician and holistic health coach inspiring others to realize their highest potential through reestablishing the integral relationship between their life and the natural world. Creating a profound partnership between horse and client Dr. Cook gently guides people of all ages, child and adult, through a profound and life transforming healing process to over come everything from eating disorders and allergies to gastrointestinal disorders, autoimmune disease and cancer.

Dr. Cook lives her medicine in every aspect of her life, residing on five acres of farm land on the banks of the Gallatin river nestled between the mountain peaks of Bozeman, Montana. There with her husband, four horses, thirteen chickens and two Labrador retrievers she practices sustainable living, raising her own food, and generously sharing of her knowledge and expertise inviting her community to experience themselves as they never have before enjoying a glass of wine at sunset on the back porch of her rustic log home.

When not practicing the natural healing arts Dr. Cook can be found mucking stalls, planting seedlings, harvesting beats, or butchering her own steaks fully savoring all the delicious richness a well lived, abundant life can offer.

RESOURCES

Cooking Resources

Books and Magazines

Nourishing Traditions: The Cookbook that Challenges Politically Correct Nutrition and the Diet Dictocrats, by Sally Fallon (1999)
Part textbook on nutrition, part cookbook with recipes from a traditional way of eating nearly lost in today's culture.

Jamie's Kitchen: A Cooking Course for Everyone, by Jamie Oliver (2003) http://www.jamieoliver.com/
Simple, innovative recipes using fresh ingredients, along with great cooking tips and techniques.

The Complete Meat Cookbook, by Bruce Aidells and Denis Kelly (2001)
The title says it all. This was my bible as I left a lifetime of vegetarianism for life as an omnivore.

Recipes from a Kitchen Garden, by Renee Shepherd and Fran Raboff (1994)
Organized by vegetable, this book is a must-have resource when the tomatoes come in and you can't figure out what to do with all ten bushels at once.

Bentley Farm Cookbook, by Virginia Bentley (1975)
A cookbook diary, beautifully handwritten and illustrated.

Cook's Illustrated magazine: http://www.cooksillustrated.com/

We have got to give a nod to the vegetarian cookbooks of our past, as they taught us so much about the use of spices and how to cook vegetables:

Passionate Vegetarian, by Crescent Dragonwagon (2002)

Vegetarian Times Complete Cookbook, by Lucy Moll and Vegetarian Times (2005, but I grew up as a cook with the 1995 edition)

Health and Nutrition Resources

Books

Nourishing Traditions: The Cookbook that Challenges Politically Correct Nutrition and the Diet Dictocrats, by Sally Fallon (1999)

The Vegetarian Myth: Food, Justice, and Sustainability, by Lierre Keith (2009)

Books by Michael Pollan:
Food Rules: An Eaters Manifesto (2009)
In Defense of Food: An Eater's Manifesto (2009)
The Omnivore's Dilemma: A Natural History of Four Meals (2007)

The Cholesterol Myths: Exposing The Fallacy That Saturated Fats and Cholesterol Cause Heart Disease, by Uffe Ravnskov, MD, PhD (2000)

The Mood Cure: The 4-Step Program to Rebalance Your Emotional Chemistry and Rediscover Your Natural Sense of Well-Being, by Julia Ross (2002)

The Whole Soy Story: The Dark Side of America's Favorite Health Food, by Kaayla T. Daniel, PhD, CCN (2005)

Nutrition and Physical Degeneration: A Comparison of Primitive and Modern Diets and Their Effects, by Weston A. Price, MS, DDS, FAGD (1939). The whole book is online at: http://journeytoforever.org/farm_library/price/pricetoc.html

Healthier Without Wheat: A New Understanding of Wheat Allergies, Celiac Disease, and Non-Celiac Gluten Intolerance, by Stephan Wagner, ND (2009)

Web sites

www.westonaprice.com
The Weston A Price Foundation was founded by Sally Fallon. The foundation aims to educate the public about Price's work and the primacy of traditional animal source foods to human health.

www.moodcure.com
Julia Ross extensively studied the connection between nutrition and mental health.

www.eatwild.com
The clearinghouse for information about pasture-based farming and the benefits of pasture feeding to animals, the Earth, and us.

www.localharvest.org
Find locally grown produce anywhere in the country. Use their map to locate farmers markets, family farms, CSAs (community-supported agriculture groups), farm stands, and "u-pick" produce in your area.

www.realmilk.com
A resource for information on raw milk and where you can source it in your area.

www.mercola.com
Great source of health articles, optimal wellness products, and free natural health newsletters with top medical news by Dr. Joseph Mercola.

www.ewg.org/foodnews
The 2011 shoppers guide to pesticides in produce. Current lists of the most and least toxic conventionally farmed produce know as the "dirty dozen" and the "clean fifteen".

RESOURCES

www.youtube.com/watch?v=dBnniua6-oM
An incredibly informative video, The Biter Truth, by Robert H. Lustig, MD, UCSF Professor of Pediatrics in the Division of Endocrinology, who explores the damage caused by sugary foods. He argues that fructose (too much) and fiber (not enough) appear to be cornerstones of the obesity epidemic through their effects on insulin.

Movies

Food, Inc. (2008)
King Corn (2007)
Fast Food Nation (2007)
The Future of Food (2004)
Super Size Me (2004)

Product Resources

Gluten Free

www.freefromgluten.com
Free from Gluten is the largest online marketplace to find gluten-free foods and products.

www.pamelasproducts.com
Pamela's gluten-free baking mixes. Personal favorites are the pancake mix and bread mix.

www.bobsredmill.com
Bob's Red Mill Natural Foods: whole grain, gluten-free, and organic foods for every meal of the day!

www.namastefoods.com
Food products that contain no wheat, gluten, corn, soy, potato, dairy, casein, tree nuts, or peanuts.

www.thecravingsplace.com
Cake, cookie, and pancake mixes free of gluten, wheat, dairy, egg, and nuts.

Coconut Milk

www.turtlemountain.com
Makers of So Delicious Coconut Milk™ beverage and nondairy ice cream.

www.coconutbliss.com
Luna and Larry's Coconut Bliss™ nondairy ice cream.

Pasture Butter

www.organicvalley.coop/products/butter/pasture/
Organic butter made from cream from grass-fed, pasture-raised cows.
www.pastureland.coop/
Grass-fed dairy cooperative in southern Minnesota producing artisan cheese and butter.

www.kerrygoldusa.com/products/butter/
Kerrygold Salted Butter is a great all-purpose, European-style butter made from grass-fed cows' milk.

Local Meats and Produce
www.localharvest.org/
Use this Web site to find farmers' markets, family farms, and other sources of sustainably grown food in your area where you can buy produce, grass-fed meats, and many other goodies.

www.eatwild.com/
Your source for safe, healthy, natural, and nutritious grass-fed beef, lamb, goat, bison, poultry, pork, dairy, and other wild edibles.

Alternative Health Care Resources

Find a naturopath in your area
American Association of Naturopathic Physicians, www.aanp.com

Naturopathic Schools

Association of Accredited Naturopathic Medical Colleges.
http://www.aanmc.org/

Food Allergy Blood Tests

Genova Diagnositics, http://www.gdx.net/

US Biotek, http://www.usbiotek.com/

Printed in Great Britain
by Amazon

85758843R00121